THE NEW SAGA LIBRARY

GENERAL EDITOR: HERMANN PÁLSSON

Eyrbyggja Saga

EYRBYGGJA SAGA

TRANSLATED BY HERMANN PÁLSSON
AND PAUL EDWARDS

Southside

EDINBURGH

1973

SOUTHSIDE (PUBLISHERS) LTD.

6 Sciennes Gardens

Edinburgh EH9 INR

UNESCO

COLLECTION OF REPRESENTATIVE WORKS

ICELANDIC SERIES

This work has been accepted in the Icelandic Translations series of the
United Nations Educational, Scientific, and Cultural Organisation
(UNESCO)

First published in Great Britain
by Southside (Publishers) Ltd.
Edinburgh 1973

Cased S.B.N. 90002506 9
Paperback S.B.N. 90002507 7

First published in Canada and the United States
by University of Toronto Press
Toronto and Buffalo 1973

Cased I.S.B.N. 0–8020–1942–0
Microfiche I.S.B.N. 0–8020–0286–2

Printed in Great Britain
by Neill & Co. Ltd
212 Causewayside
Edinburgh EH9 IPP
Scotland

DEDICATED TO

Dr Kristján Eldjárn

PRESIDENT OF

ICELAND

Contents

EYRBYGGJA SAGA

CONTENTS

CONTENTS

Introduction

WRITING IN 1813, SIR WALTER SCOTT says that "of all the various records of Icelandic history and literature, there is none more interesting than *Eyrbyggja Saga*".[1] It is not surprising that a novelist as fascinated by the past as Scott should so respond to the world of *Eyrbyggja Saga*, which indeed is in many respects akin to that of the romantic imagination. There are antiquarian elements, such as the detailed (though largely invented) description of the temple at Thor's Ness and of the duties of a pagan priesthood; there are gothic elements, such as the eerie hauntings at Frodriver and the unquiet graves of the malevolent dead; and along with these there are violent encounters with vikings and berserks and a pervasive heroic spirit. But the author of the Waverley Novels must have been still more powerfully fascinated by the elaborate structure of a narrative in which the lives of many remarkable and varied individuals are set against a background of actual historical events to produce an imaginative view of history. For it must be stressed at once that although the saga often seems to be recording history, its true spirit is imaginative and interpretative, a thirteenth-century view of the past.

On the surface, *Eyrbyggja Saga* reads like an historical record, tracing the lives of several generations from the late ninth century to the early eleventh. The narrative opens with the pagan anarchy of the Viking Age, but moves rapidly to an account of the settlement of Iceland and the beginnings of an organised society. A

---

1. W. Scott, "Abstract of the Eyrbyggja Saga" in Mallet's *Illustrations of Northern Antiquities* (1814).

11

period of internal strain and violence, as the laws are hammered out on the lives of proud and inflexible individuals, closes with the arrival of Christianity and the gradual establishment of the ordered civilisation of medieval Iceland. Later we shall examine the artistic pattern of the saga in some detail and shall have more to say about its historical framework: at this point, however, we might generalise and say that *Eyrbyggja Saga* describes a community progressing from lawlessness to collective responsibility. But by the time the saga was written Icelandic society was both politically and economically in decline, and so the saga is essentially nostalgic, reflecting pride in the past rather than in the author's own times.

The precise date and provenance of *Eyrbyggja Saga* are matters for speculation; and, as with the other Sagas of Icelanders, its author is unknown. All the same, it seems likely that it was composed not long after the middle of the thirteenth century, and quite probably at Helgafell, the focal place of the story. It is tempting to speculate that it may have been written in the Augustinian house which was founded at Helgafell in 1184 and was an important intellectual centre and scriptorium right through to the end of the medieval period. A number of manuscripts still extant were written by priests who were either inmates of the house, or had been trained there. Two of the heads of the house were direct descendants of Snorri the Priest, the main figure of *Eyrbyggja Saga*: these were Thorfinn Thorgeirsson (1188–1216) and Ketil Hermundarson (1217–30). It was at Helgafell, too, that Ari Thorgilsson the Learned, Iceland's first vernacular historian, was born. There was a considerable library there of nearly 120 books around the year 1186, and towards the end of the fourteenth century about 120 books in Latin and 35 in Icelandic. It has been suggested that *Laxdæla Saga* and *Eyrbyggja Saga* were composed at about the same time by two members of the house at Helgafell, and that they used each other's work, for each saga shows knowledge of the other. This would explain why Helgafell becomes the focal place of *Laxdœla Saga* precisely at the point where it ceases to be that of *Eyrbyggja Saga*.[2]

The structure of the saga is so complicated that many readers have compared it unfavourably with *Njal's Saga, Gisli's Saga*, above all *Grettir's Saga*, in which the hero's life is so central to the narrative that it provides a clearly-defined structural core, no matter what the surrounding complexities may be. However, once *Eyrbyggja Saga* is read in its own terms, rather than in terms of the organisation of other, deceptively similar sagas, distinct patterns begin to emerge. These patterns display an inter-relation of families and individuals in two dimensions. First there is the linear movement from the ninth to the eleventh century, from the first settlers to their great-grandchildren. Then there are all the complex social relationships between these people living in a small community, bound by duties often arising out of marriage ties, or out of enmities caused by the grabbing of land or the killing of a kinsman. The pattern could best be illustrated by guiding the reader initially through the events of the saga and pointing out the landmarks. The saga might be broken down into eight sections, as follows:

1. *Prologue* (Chs. 1–8). This describes the rise of Harald Fine-Hair, King of Norway, and the pressure placed upon certain powerful and rebellious

---

2. Late in *Eyrbyggja Saga* (Ch. 56) we are told that "in the spring Snorri exchanged farms with Gudrun, Osvif's daughter . . . ". *Laxdœla Saga* (Ch. 56) records Gudrun's move to Helgafell.

chieftains and landowners who are unwilling to accept Harald's rule. Under these pressures a number of them leave Norway, some going to the newly-discovered, uninhabited land called Iceland. Two of these in particular are described, Thorolf Mostur-Beard and Bjorn the Easterner. Thorolf is a priest of Thor, and establishes strict rules of conduct:

> Thorolf gave the name Thor's Ness to the region between Vigra Fjord and Hofsvag. On this headland is a mountain held so sacred by Thorolf that no-one was allowed even to look at it without first having washed himself, and no living creatures on this mountain, neither men nor beasts, were to be harmed unless they left it of their own accord. Thorolf called this mountain Helga Fell and believed that he and his kinsmen would go into it when they died.
>
> Thorolf used to hold all his courts on the point of the headland where Thor had come ashore, and that was where he started the district assembly. This place was so holy that he wouldn't let anyone desecrate it either with bloodshed or with excrement; and for privy purposes they used a special rock in the sea which they called Dritsker [lit. 'Dirt Skerry'].[3]

Bjorn's respect for the old gods is also made clear, and at this point in the narrative there is no reason to expect anything but friendship between the descendants of these two founder-fathers.

2. *Quarrels between Thorsnessings and Kjalleklings* (Chs. 9–28). In the next generation, however, trouble begins between the people of Thor's Ness, who are descendants of Thorolf, called the Thorsnessings, and the sons of Kjallak, who are Bjorn the Easterner's grand-children. Both families have become very powerful, and family pride leads to conflict.

3. Below, p. 41.

Quarrels begin over what might appear at first sight a trivial matter, the refusal of the Kjalleklings to go out to Dritsker to ease themselves. But the descendants of Thorolf take their attempted desecration of the holy place very seriously indeed, and tensions build up, in spite of efforts at peace-making, to a series of clashes. In due course a battle is fought between the followers of Thorarin the Black (related by marriage to the Kjalleklings) and Thorbjorn the Stout (related by marriage to Snorri the Priest, descendant of Thorolf Mostur-Beard). Once again the basis of the quarrel, the alleged theft of some horses, hardly seems to justify the bitterness of feelings and the killings that follow. But the very triviality of the surface causes of conflict only serves to emphasise the undercurrent of unreasoning pride and smouldering neurotic violence. This particular sequence of quarrels slowly resolves itself, mainly as a result of the skilful manœuvrings of Snorri, who ends up giving advice and aid over two troublesome berserks belonging to Styr, one of the leading men of the Kjallekling clan. The berserks are killed; Snorri marries Styr's daughter; Thorarin the Black goes overseas and is, we are told, "now out of the story." This, however, is only a lull, and a new set of tensions has already begun to develop, to explode into violence in the next part of the story. Indeed, the enmity between the descendants of Thorolf and those of Bjorn rears up from under the surface of many a subsequent conflict.

3. *The Conflict between Snorri and Arnkel* (Chs. 29–38). Arnkel is the virtuous but strong-minded son of a malicious viking settler, Thorolf Twist-Foot, and, like Snorri, a great man and a temple priest. Since he and Snorri are the two greatest men in the district, people with lawsuits naturally come to them for guidance and support. The seeds of conflict have earlier been sown over Snorri's killing of a man called Vigfus. With the support of the Kjalleklings, Arnkel had taken up the case against Snorri on behalf of Vigfus' kin. Now once again it seems that pride and honour will not allow two cocks to crow in the same district. Arnkel had

inherited the fighting qualities of his viking father, without his malice, but he also has the generosity of spirit shown by his grandmother Geirrid:

> She built a hall right across the road, so that every traveller had to ride through it. In the hall stood a table, always laden with food, and everyone was welcome to share it. Because of this, people thought her a very remarkable woman indeed.[4]

It is inevitable that a man as great-hearted and as firm-minded as Arnkel should come into conflict with the cunning and ambivalent Snorri, about whom we shall have more to say in due course. In his purity of motive and his strength of purpose, Arnkel is what Snorri is to become in the later stages of the narrative. Tensions culminate in the heroic last stand of Arnkel, alone against Snorri and his blood-brothers, the trouble-making Thorbrandssons. Arnkel is killed, but his death is lamented as a great loss, and as an indication of what is wrong with this society:

> Arnkel was mourned by everyone, for of all men in pagan times he was the most gifted. He was outstandingly shrewd in judgment, good-tempered, kind-hearted, brave, honest, and moderate. He came out on top in every law-suit, no matter who he was dealing with, and that is why people were so envious of him, as the manner of his death proves.[5]

Since Arnkel leaves no male heir to take legal action over his killing, Snorri gets off very lightly. That the death of a man as outstanding as Arnkel should be so neglected in law is seen as a social disgrace, and the author makes the point that in consequence the law was changed. So we are made aware of the growing social responsibility underlying all the

---

4. Below, p. 45.   5. Below, pp. 124–5.

violence and pride. However, another sequence has been completed, Arnkel is dead, and Snorri's power continues to increase.

4. *Snorri and the Thorbrandssons versus Bjorn and the Thorlakssons* (Chs. 39–48). Yet another set of enmities has been developing during the previous sequence of events. Snorri's blood-brothers, the Thorbrandssons, who aided him in the attack on Arnkel, are now in conflict with a group called the Thorlakssons, who are living at Eyr. Snorri is also at odds with a man from Breidavik, Bjorn Asbrandsson, who has been having an affair with Snorri's married sister Thurid. It is generally known, though apparently not talked about, that Thurid's son, Kjartan, is the child of Bjorn, not of her husband Thorodd. In his disgrace, Thorodd has appealed to Snorri for help, so that now these new conflicting groups are ranged against one another. The surface causes of tension are as usual quite trivial – a blow with a hot porridge-ladle, a piece of turf thrown in a game – but the cuckolding of Thorodd sharpens the tension; Snorri secretly sends a slave on a mission to kill one of the men of Breidavik; Bjorn and his brother catch and kill the slave; and once more violence breaks out. There are two major battles, Alfta Fjord and Vigra Fjord, and the strain which is being put on society is clearly marked by the dilemma of Styr, who is not only a Kjallekling, related to the Thorlakssons, and so tied by blood to Snorri's enemies, but is also Snorri's father-in-law, and indebted to him for help given against the troublesome berserks. At the Battle of Alfta Fjord, Styr is fighting on the side of his kinsmen the Thorlakssons against Snorri. But when Snorri's twelve-year-old son (and so Styr's own grandson) is wounded, Snorri exaggerates, telling Styr that the boy is dying:

[Styr] was the one to claim the first victim when he killed one of the supporters of his own son-in-law, Snorri. When Snorri saw this he asked, 'Is this how you avenge your grandson Thorodd when he's dying of the wound Steinthor gave him? You're no better than a traitor!'

'I can soon make it up to you,' said Styr, and with that he changed sides. He joined Snorri with all his followers, and the next man he killed was one of Steinthor's. [6]

Yet again the author draws attention to the enormous pressure these conflicts are placing on society. In due course, peace terms are agreed – "The killings by Styr, one on each side, cancelled each other out," we are told – but the matter of Bjorn's affair with Thurid is still to be settled. In a brilliant dramatic episode Snorri sets out to kill Bjorn, dressed in the blue cloak characteristically worn by the killer in the sagas:

Bjorn watched the riders coming down from the moor into the meadow and recognised them at once. Snorri the Priest was in the lead wearing a blue cloak. Then Bjorn made a daring move. He picked up the knife and walked straight up to them. When he got to Snorri, he took hold of his cloak-sleeve with one hand and pointed the knife right at Snorri's chest with the other, ready to drive it home at once. Bjorn greeted them, and Snorri returned his greeting, but Mar lost his nerve when he saw how easily Bjorn could stab Snorri if anyone tried to rush him. Bjorn walked them on their way and asked the news, but he didn't relax the firm grip he had on Snorri. [7]

Still, Snorri gets his way without violence, for he manages to persuade Bjorn to leave Iceland; and so Bjorn is to all intents "out of the story", though he is to reappear right at the end of the narrative in a brief, mysterious episode set in an unknown land across the sea.

---

6. Below, p. 143.   7. Below, p. 153.

5. *Christianity and the Ghosts* (Chs. 49–55). Christianity now reaches
Iceland, and the mode of the story undergoes certain changes. It is Snorri,
lawyer, warrior, killer, priest of Thor, who now does more than anyone
to persuade the Icelanders to embrace Christianity. There is an enter-
taining episode in which two women briefly take a central place in the
story: Thorgunna, a rich, middle-aged immigrant from the Hebrides, and
Thurid, Bjorn's mistress and Snorri's sister, who has taken a liking to
Thorgunna's fine clothes and splendid bed-furnishings. But the tone of
the episode grows increasingly ominous as Thorgunna's death introduces
a series of hauntings which have been hinted at earlier in the death and
burial of Arnkel's evil-hearted viking father, Thorolf Twist-Foot. Now
the ghosts of old Iceland take the centre of the stage, confronting the new
religion. There are a number of echoes from the pagan past; Thorodd and
the drowned men who visit the Christmas home-fires of Frodriver will
remind the reader of the fires and feasting of the drowned Thorstein
the Cod-Biter and his men inside the holy mountain of Helga Fell early
on in the story. [8] But Snorri gives advice, and the ghosts are banished by a
striking combination, the old law and the new religion. First of all the
ghosts are summoned to a "door-court" and leave reluctantly when they
are found legally guilty of trespassing. Then prayers are said, holy water
is sprinkled, and the land is disinfected of its unholy past. But there is
another element of the pagan past which has to be exorcised along with
the ghosts, and that is the world of the vikings, the violence and crime that
have bedevilled society's struggle towards order. This is the subject of the
next episode.

6. *Snorri against Ospak and the Vikings* (Chs. 56–62). A viking called
Ospak begins to raid and kill, grabbing loot wherever he and his men can

---

8. Below, p. 51.

lay hands on it, and causing havoc in the farming community, where people are neither powerful enough nor violent enough to defend themselves effectively against this arbitrary onslaught from the past. At first Snorri, characteristically, does little but wait – "he let people talk" – but the crafty lawyer and killer has been undergoing a slow change towards social responsibility. He now acts on behalf of society against lawlessness, leading the farmers in battle against the outlaws, killing their leaders and coming to terms with the rest.

7. *Echoes from the Past* (Chs. 63–64). The scene is set for the dying cadences of the narrative, remembrances of the past as it fades with a distant rumble of the ancient thunder. The blackened, uncorrupted corpse of the villainous Thorolf Twist-Leg rises from his grave, and is the last of the ghosts to be laid, taking with him Thorodd Thorbrandsson, another old trouble-maker, a survivor of the Battle of Vigra Fjord and one of Snorri's companions in the killing of Thorolf Twist-Foot's son, the noble Arnkel. As Thorolf's spirit, in the form of a demonic bull, takes the life of the farmer Thorodd and vanishes for ever into a swamp, distant echoes of jealousy and violence fade from the narrative. An entirely new figure, Gudleif, meets a mysterious old chieftain in a strange, undefined country where his ship has been driven in a storm, and it turns out that this is none other than Bjorn, the lover of Thurid and father of Kjartan. But he will not declare his name openly, insists that no-one must ever visit him – indeed they cannot, for the land where he lives is never precisely located – and vanishes from the naturalistic part of the narrative just as Thorolf's ghost has vanished from the supernaturalistic.

8. *Epilogue* (Ch. 65). The narrative from which Snorri has emerged as the principal figure, illustrative of the best and the worst, growing in stature throughout the story, ends with the listing of his kin, his sons, his daughters, their children, and the farms on which they live. But the bones of the dead no longer rise to create trouble amongst the living:

Snorri the Priest died at Sælingsdale Tongue a year after the killing of King Olaf the Saint, and was buried at the church he himself had built. When the graveyard there was changed, his bones were removed to the site of the present church. Gudny, Bodvar's Daughter, was present, the mother of the Sturlusons, Snorri, Thord, and Sighvat, and she said that Snorri the Priest's bones were those of a man of average height, not very tall. She also said that the bones of Snorri's uncle, Bork the Stout, had been dug up and that they were exceptionally big. The bones of old Thordis, Sur's Daughter, were dug up too, and Gudny said they were those of a small woman, and black as if they had been singed. All these bones were buried again at the place where the church now stands. [9]

Snorri has been the outstanding, most ambivalent figure in the story. His very name means "turbulent" and is given him in place of his original name Thorgrim because he is "a very difficult child". He is born in violence, for only a few days before his birth, his father is killed in the course of a vendetta by Gisli, the hero of *Gisli's Saga*. Snorri's mother Thordis marries his father's brother, Bork, and as in the story of Hamlet there are further tensions here. Snorri takes sides with his mother against his step-father, and indeed husband and wife are locked in conflict, for Gisli, the killer of Snorri's father, is also the brother of Thordis, his mother, and she, like her son, is torn between conflicting duties. Snorri exhibits contradictory impulses throughout his life. He can fight bravely and honourably, but he is also capable of sending a criminal to kill his enemy by stealth. He is a peace-maker one moment, a man of blood the next. The narrator regularly speculates on Snorri's

---

9. Below, p. 198.

motives: at one point, when Snorri is making peace, the narrator adds that people believe Snorri only did so because he saw distant reinforcements on the way to join his opponents. The Thorbrandssons send a slave, Egil, to kill Bjorn and his brother, but the narrator adds that "some people think Snorri the Priest was behind the plot." Snorri is a pagan priest, yet does more than anyone to persuade the Icelanders to embrace Christianity. Though he emerges from the tale as a distinct personality, little about that personality is unambiguous, as the narrator suggests in his description of Snorri:

> Snorri was a man of medium height and rather slight build, a handsome, regular-featured man with a fair complexion, flaxen hair, and a reddish beard. He was usually even-tempered, and it wasn't easy to tell whether he was pleased or not. He was a very shrewd man with remarkable foresight, a long memory, and a taste for vengeance. To his friends he was a sound adviser, but his enemies learned to fear the advice he gave. As Snorri was now in charge of the temple he was called Snorri the Priest. He became a man of great power, and some people envied him bitterly, . . .[10]

In fact, he is the very epitome both of the stresses within early Icelandic society, and of its growth from lawlessness to order and discipline. To Walter Scott, Snorri was the most fascinating figure in the most fascinating of sagas:

> That such a character, partaking more of the jurisconsult or statesman than of the warrior, should have risen so high in such an early period, argues the preference which the Icelanders already

---

10. Below, p. 58.

assigned to mental superiority over the rude attributes of strength and courage, and furnishes another proof of the early civilization of this extraordinary commonwealth.[11]

E Y R B Y G G J A   S A G A, OF COURSE, WAS NOT CREATED in a vacuum, and it belongs to the main stream of medieval Icelandic literary tradition. As we have said, it was probably written shortly after the middle of the thirteenth century at a time when many sagas had already been composed. The author uses a number of written sources: several chapters derive from the *Book of Settlements* (*Landnámabók*), probably the version, now lost, of Styrmir Kárason (d. 1245). The earliest extant version of the *Book of Settlements*, that of Sturla Thordarson (1214–84) in turn added material taken from *Eyrbyggja Saga*, and so one text cross-fertilises another. Several sagas are referred to in *Eyrbyggja Saga*: Ch. 24 gives a summary of part of *Eirik's Saga*;[12] the killing of Snorri's father and other elements in the story refer to *Gisli's Saga*; and the author also uses *Laxdæla Saga*[13] and *Heidarviga Saga*. Thus, while *Eyrbyggja Saga* draws upon historical records, it also belongs to the great tradition of story-telling, and must be seen as fictionalised history. It would be a mistake to think of it as a factual historical account, and elements of authorial fancy can

---

11. Scott, *Illustrations of Northern Antiquities.*

12. In *The Vinland Sagas*, tr. M. Magnusson & H. Pálsson, Penguin Classics, Harmondsworth 1963.

13. *Laxdæla Saga*, tr. M. Magnusson & H. Pálsson, Penguin Classics, Harmondsworth 1969.

easily be demonstrated. At the same time, it is useful to see the framework of chronology upon which the events of the tale are founded, as they are recorded in the *Icelandic Annals*:

874	Ingolf Arnarson goes to Iceland.[14]
918	Thorolf Mostur-Beard dies.
938	Thorgrim the Priest (father of Snorri) is born.
952	Thorbjorn Sur (father of Thordis, Snorri's mother) comes to Iceland.
963	Thorgrim the Priest is killed, Snorri is born.
986	Eirik the Red colonises Greenland.
1000	Christianity is adopted by law.
1008	Styr (Snorri's father-in-law) is killed.
1031	Snorri dies.
1112	Thurid Snorri's-daughter dies aged 88.

Well-informed people like old Thurid would offer the twelfth-century Icelandic historian a long unbroken link with the past; and she was in fact one of the informants of Ari the Learned (1068–1148), author of the *Book of Icelanders* (*Íslendingabók*) and co-author of the first version of the Book of Settlements. As already mentioned, a later version of the latter was probably used by the author of *Eyrbyggja Saga;* and his imaginative and inventive powers would be able to play with confidence upon such firmly based history and chronology as this and the *Icelandic Annals*.

As we have already observed, the author, however, takes pleasure in the antiquarian as well as in the more specifically

---

14. Cp. *Eyrbyggja Saga* (Ch. 3: below, p. 38), of Thorolf Mostur-Beard's emigration: "This was ten years after Ingolf Arnarson had sailed off to settle in Iceland."

historical. His attempt to describe the temple of Thor illustrates the fascination which the past held for the thirteenth-century Icelander much better than it records pagan customs, and indeed when we come to the great hauntings at Frodriver it is apparent that the author's gothic imagination is excitedly at work. Again and again, however, we hear such phrases as "it was the law in those days", or "as people did in those days", or "according to ancient custom". The author is interested in omens, in the speaking head on Geirvor, in the black cloud that rains blood before the death of Thorgunna, and he regularly organises scenes in such a way that they have a quality of inevitability which is splendid drama, but hardly acceptable as history. But he is interested, too, in the actual physical landmarks of the past: of the berserks' wall he says, "you can still see traces of it"; of Thor's Stone, "you can still see the blood on the stone"; of the wall built behind Thorolf Twist-Foot's grave, "you can still see traces of the wall there". The geography is another accurately-recorded feature, and a strong contributory factor to the impression of realism is the description of everyday activities, of farming and fishing, tools, techniques, and the organisation of domestic routines. Though in some respects the world of *Eyrbyggja Saga* was remote from that of its author - the vikings, the old gods, the witchcraft, for example – in others it was still close, for the methods of farming, the kind of homes people lived in, the assemblies they attended, were still much the same. But perhaps more than anything else, the delineation of character persuades us of the reality of this mixed world of the marvellous and the commonplace, the historically accurate and the artfully designed.

We have seen already in the case of Snorri how the author is interested in complexities of character and the relationship of character to background. The virtuous Arnkel, Snorri's opponent in a major section of the narrative, is more simply drawn, but even here one recognises the author's sense, not only of what men inherit from their parents, but also of what they reject. Arnkel inherits his father's best qualities as a fighting man, but reacts against his malicious trouble-making, inheriting the generosity and openness of his grandmother Geirrid, who built her hall across the road and had tables ready laden with food for hungry travellers. Thorolf Twist-Foot himself can be seen as reacting against the best qualities of his mother:

> Thorolf thought that the lands which his mother had taken were not nearly big enough, so he challenged Ulfar the Champion to single combat for the lands he owned, Ulfar being old and childless.[15]

And the narrator tells us that Thorolf "was a very hard man". So tensions within the family are being established which will not only become crucial to the development of the plot, but also lead to acute observations on human conduct. Thorolf tries to persuade Arnkel to take action against Snorri over a stretch of woodland. Arnkel refuses, even though he wishes to take action (and indeed does so after his father's death), simply because his father urges it, and he must react against him. Thorolf goes off home in a rage, and appropriately it seems to be rage that he dies of:

> Thorolf went back home in a fury because he could see how difficult it was going to be for him to get what he wanted. It was evening when he got back and he sat down on the high-seat without uttering

---

15. Below, p. 45.

a word to anybody. He didn't eat all evening and stayed in his seat
when the rest of the household went to bed. In the morning, when
they got up, Thorolf was still sitting there, dead.[16]

The author's pleasure in less grim aspects of character can be
seen in the relationship between Thurid and Thorgunna, with
Thurid unable to keep her eyes, and ultimately her hands, off
Thorgunna's fine and fashionable clothes and her magnificent
bedding. Thorgunna herself, by no means a major figure in the
story, is splendidly presented:

> Thorgunna spent every day weaving, unless there was hay-
> making to do; and when the weather was good, she used to work at
> drying the hay in the home meadow. She had a special rake made for
> her and wouldn't let anyone else touch it. Thorgunna was a massive
> woman, tall, broadly built, and getting very stout. She had dark
> eyebrows and narrow eyes, and beautiful chestnut hair. Her manner
> was always very proper, and she used to go to mass every morning
> before starting work, but she wasn't easy to get on with and didn't
> waste much time on conversation. People thought she must be in
> her fifties, though she was still a very active woman.[17]

The last sentence particularly takes on a sharper significance when
we learn that Thorgunna has taken a fancy to someone:

> Kjartan the farmer's son was the only one there Thorgunna took to,
> and she liked him a lot: but he kept his distance, which she used to
> find very irritating. Kjartan was fourteen or fifteen at the time, a big
> lad, and very manly.[18]

---

16. Below, p. 114.   17. Below, p. 158.   18. Below, p. 158.

This domineering, irascible, aging, still sexually excitable woman with a cradle-snatching crush on a teenager is delineated here in a few neat, precise strokes. It seems appropriate that when the dead Thorgunna is being taken some distance for burial, her corpse should rise up and cook a meal for the coffin-bearers, stark naked, and as domineering as ever. Her interest in Kjartan has its comic side, but the narrator refuses to stress this at Thorgunna's expense, as a less detached artist might have done, and leaves it to us to be amused, to feel superior, to sympathise, even to moralise, if we will. His responsibility is to convey with charity, understanding, and economy an interesting and essentially open situation, to stir, but not to rule, his reader's imagination and judgment.

THE PRESENT TRANSLATION IS BASED on Einar Ólafur Sveinsson's standard edition in *Íslenzk Fornrit*, Vol. IV (1935). There are four earlier versions of *Eyrbyggja Saga* in English. The first of these is the adaptation made by Sir Walter Scott in 1813. Scott's version, based on Grímur Thorkelin's Latin translation of 1787, was printed in *Illustrations of Northern Antiquities* in 1814. Under the title *The Ere-Dwellers* the saga was then translated by William Morris and Eiríkr Magnússon, in the Saga Library, Vol. II (1892). Guðbrandr Vigfússon and F. York Powell offered a translation of the saga in their *Origines Islandicae*, Vols. I–II (1905). Finally, it was translated by Paul Schach (with an introduction and verse translations by Lee M. Hollander): *Eyrbyggja Saga*, Nebraska 1959.

We should like to add our thanks to Mrs Betty Radice for reading the typescript and making many helpful suggestions, and to

Mr R. L. C. Lorimer of Southside (Publishers) Ltd for his careful editorial scrutiny of the final version of the text.

Finally we wish to thank President Kristján Eldjárn for kindly allowing us to dedicate this volume to him.

Edinburgh
November 1972

HERMANN PÁLSSON
PAUL EDWARDS

List of Characters

1: THE THORSNESSINGS

THOROLF MOSTUR-BEARD	*a settler from Norway*
THORSTEIN THE COD-BITER	*founder of Helgafell, his son*
BORK THE STOUT THORGRIM THE PRIEST	*sons of Thorstein the Cod-Biter*
THORDIS	*wife of Thorgrim, and later married to Bork*
SNORRI THE PRIEST	*son of Thorgrim and Thordis*
THURID	*daughter of Bork and Thordis; second wife of Thorbjorn the Stout of Frodriver*

2: THE KJALLEKLINGS

BJORN THE EASTERNER	*of Bjorn's Haven, a settler from Norway*
KJALLAK THE OLD HELGA, wife of Asgeir of Eyr	*his children*
THORGRIM THE PRIEST	*of Bjorn's Haven, son of Kjallak the Old*
VERMUND THE SLENDER, of Bjorn's Haven KILLER-STYR, of Hraun	*sons of Thorgrim*
VIGFUS OF DRAPUHLID	*a distant relative*

31

3: ARNKEL'S FAMILY

GEIRROD	*a settler*
GEIRRID	*of Borgardale, his sister*
THOROLF TWIST-FOOT	*of Hvamm, her son*
ARNKEL THE PRIEST, of Bolstad GEIRRID OF MAVAHLID	*children of Thorolf Twist-Foot*
THORGERD	*their niece, wife of Vigfus of Drapuhlid*
THORARIN THE BLACK GUDNY, wife of Killer-Styr	*children of Geirrid of Mavahlid*

4: THE MEN OF EYR

VESTAR	*a settler*
ASGEIR	*his son*
THORLAK	*son of Asgeir*
STEINTHOR THORMOD BERGTHOR THORD BLIG	*sons of Thorlak*

5: THE MEN OF BREIDAVIK

ASBRAND OF KAMB

BJORN the Breidavik ⎫
champion ⎪
ARINBJORN THE STRONG ⎬ *his children*
THURID, first wife of ⎪
Thorbjorn the Stout of Frodriver ⎭

GUNNLAUG *son of Thorbjorn and Thurid*

6: THE MEN OF ALFTAFJORD

FINNGEIR *a settler*

THORFINN *his son*

THORBRAND *son of Thorfinn*

THORLEIF KIMBI ⎫
SNORRI ⎪
⎬ *sons of Thorbrand*
THORODD ⎪
THORFINN ⎭

FREYSTEIN BOFI *foster son of Thorbrand*

EYRBYGGJA SAGA

CHAPTER I

Ketil Flat-Nose

THERE WAS A GREAT CHIEFTAIN in Norway called Ketil Flat-Nose, the son of Bjorn Buna, son of Grim, one of the leading men in Sogn. Ketil was married to Yngvild, the daughter of Ketil Wether, a chieftain in Romerike. Their sons were Bjorn and Helgi, and their daughters Aud the Deep-Minded, Thorunn Hyrna, and Jorunn Wisdom-Slope.[1] Bjorn Ketilsson was brought up east in Jamtaland by Earl Kjallak, a wise man and very highly thought of. Earl Kjallak had a son called Bjorn, too, as well as a daughter, Gjaflaug.

Just about that time King Harald Fine-Hair was forcing his way to power in Norway.[2] During the campaign a good many men of importance cleared out of their estates in Norway, some emigrating east across the Kjolen Mountains, some west over the North Sea. Others used to winter in the Hebrides or in Orkney, then spend the summers raiding in Harald's kingdom and doing plenty of damage there. The farmers complained about it to the King and

---

1. For Ketil Flat-Nose and his children, see also *The Book of Settlements*, Ch. 13, and *Laxdœla Saga*, tr. Magnusson and Pálsson, pp. 47–67.
2. The events described in Chs. 1–2 are evidently supposed to have occurred *c.*865–75. According to the *Icelandic Annals*, King Harald ruled for 70 years and died in 931.

asked him to get rid of these trouble-makers, so he decided to organise an expedition west over the sea, with Ketil Flat-Nose in command. Ketil tried to talk his way out of it, but the King said Ketil would have to go; and once he realised that the King was determined to have his own way, Ketil got ready for the voyage, taking his wife along and all his children who happened to be staying with him.

After having landed in the west, Ketil fought a number of battles, and won every one of them. He conquered and took over the Hebrides, making peace and alliances with all the leading men there in the west. After that, Ketil sent the troops back to Norway. When they came to King Harald, they told him all about how Ketil had taken over the Hebrides, but they couldn't say that he was doing much to bring the islands under King Harald's rule. As soon as the King heard this, he confiscated all Ketil's estates in Norway.

Ketil Flat-Nose married his daughter Aud to Olaf the White, the greatest warrior-king at that time in the British Isles. Olaf was the son of Ingjald Helgason and of Thora, daughter of Sigurd Snake-in-the-Eye, son of Ragnar Hairy-Breeks. His other daughter, Thorunn, Ketil married to Helgi the Lean, son of Eyvind the Easterner and of Rafarta, daughter of King Kjarval of Ireland.

CHAPTER 2

Bjorn is outlawed

BJORN KETILSSON STAYED ON in Jamtaland until Earl Kjallak died; then he married the Earl's daughter Gjaflaug, and after that travelled west across the Kjolen Mountains. First he went to Trondheim, then south from there to his father's estates, where he took over, and threw out the stewards King Harald had put in charge.

King Harald was in Oslo Fjord when he heard about this; and without wasting any time he set out across the mountains towards Trondheim. As soon as he got there, Harald called people together from eight provinces and formally declared Bjorn Ketilsson an outlaw in Norway, which meant that people could lawfully kill him, if they could catch him anywhere. The King sent Hauk Long-Breeks and some other warriors to execute Bjorn if they could find him, but when these men came south to Stad, Bjorn's friends got wind of their mission and warned him. So Bjorn jumped into a skiff he had and sailed off with his household and goods. Since it was the worst time of winter, he decided not to risk the open sea but kept south along the coast instead. On he sailed till he reached Mostur Island off South Hordaland. There a man called Hrolf, son of Ornolf the Fish-Driver, gave him a friendly welcome; so there Bjorn stayed on in hiding for the rest of the winter.

The King's agents went back north again as soon as they had made arrangements about Bjorn's estates and put men in charge of them.

CHAPTER 3

Thorolf Mostur-Beard

B ESIDES RUNNING A GOOD FARM, this Hrolf was a chieftain of some importance. He was a close friend of Thor's, and he was in charge of Thor's temple there on the island, so people called him Thorolf. A tall strong man, Thorolf was very handsome and his long beard got him the nickname Mostur-Beard. Thorolf was respected above all other men on the island.

In the spring Thorolf gave Bjorn a magnificent longship with a good fighting crew, and sent his son Hallstein voyaging with him. They sailed west across the North Sea and there joined up with Bjorn's kinsmen.

When King Harald heard that Thorolf Mostur-Beard had been sheltering his outlaw Bjorn Ketilsson, he sent messengers dismissing Thorolf from his estates, with the warning that unless he gave himself up and placed himself in the king's hands, he'd be outlawed like his friend Bjorn. This was ten years after Ingolf Arnarson had sailed off to settle in Iceland, a voyage that was on everyone's lips. People coming back from Iceland had nothing but good to say of it.[1]

---

1. According to Ari Thorgilsson's *Book of Icelanders* (written *c.*1125), Ingolf Arnarson, the first Norwegian to make his permanent home in Iceland, went there in 870, "about the time when St Edmund of East Anglia was martyred by the Vikings". However, the earliest extant version of the *Book of Settlements*, compiled by Sturla Thordarson (1214–84), and the *Icelandic Annals* both date Ingolf's arrival to the year 874.

CHAPTER 4

Thorolf goes to Iceland

THOROLF MOSTUR-BEARD HELD a great feast and asked
the advice of his friend Thor about what he should do, make
peace with the King, or leave the country and try his luck elsewhere. As it turned out, Thorolf was advised to go to Iceland, so he
bought a good-sized ocean-going ship, got it ready for the voyage,
and sailed off with his goods and household, as well as many of his
friends who'd decided to go with him. He dismantled the temple,
and along with most of its timbers he put aside some of the earth
from under Thor's pedestal.

Thorolf put to sea and had a good passage. He made his
landfall in the south and sailed west along the coast round Reykja
Ness. By the time the good wind began to fail them they could
make out some broad bays cutting into the coast. Thorolf threw
overboard the high-seat pillars from the temple – the figure of Thor
was carved on one of them – and declared that he'd settle at any
spot in Iceland where Thor chose to send the pillars ashore. No
sooner had the pillars begun drifting away from the ship than they
were swept towards the western bay and not at all slowly either,
from what people could see. Then a breeze sprang up, and Thorolf
sailed westward round Snæfell Ness into the bay. They could see
how broad and long it was, with high mountains on either side, so
Thorolf chose a name for it and called it Breida Fjord. He put in to
land on the south side, half-way up, and where he brought his ship
in came to be known later as Hofsvag.[1] Then he started exploring

---

1. Lit. "Temple Creek". Later, according to the story, Thorolf's temple
stood near the creek.

the land, and on the tip of the headland to the north of the creek they saw where Thor had come ashore with the pillars. It's been called Thor's Ness ever since. Thorolf carried fire round the land he claimed, between the Staf River in the west and the one he called Thor's River in the east, and there he settled his crew.[2]

Thorolf established a great farm at Hofsvag and called it Hofstad. He had a large temple built there, with its door in one of the side walls near the gable. Just inside the door stood the high-seat pillars with the so-called holy nails fixed in them, and beyond that point the whole building was considered to be a sanctuary. Inside the main temple was a structure built much like the choir in churches nowadays, and in the middle a raised platform like an altar. On this platform lay a solid ring weighing twenty ounces, upon which people had to swear all their oaths. It was the business of the temple priest to carry this ring at every public meeting. There was a sacrificial bowl on the platform too, with a sacrificial twig shaped like a priest's aspergill, with which the blood of animals killed as offerings to the gods was to be sprinkled from the bowl. Inside the choir-like part of the building the figures of gods were arranged in a circle all around the platform. Every farmer had to pay tax to the temple, and another of their duties was to support the temple priest, in just the same way as farmers nowadays have to support their chieftains. It was the priest's business to see to the temple and keep it up at his own expense, as well as to hold sacrificial feasts.[3]

---

2. The custom of carrying fire round the land claimed is mentioned several times in the *Book of Settlements*, and seems to have been intended to keep evil spirits away.   3. This is the most detailed and circumstantial description of a pagan temple and the sacerdotal functions of the priest-chieftains to be found anywhere in medieval Icelandic literature. Its authenticity, however, is rather doubtful.

Thorolf gave the name Thor's Ness to the region between **Vigra** Fjord and Hofsvag. On this headland there is a mountain held so sacred by Thorolf that no-one was allowed even to look at it without first having washed himself, and no living creatures on this mountain, neither man or beasts, were to be harmed unless they left it of their own accord. Thorolf called that mountain Helga Fell[4] and believed that he and his kinsmen would go into it when they died.[5]

Thorolf used to hold all his courts on the point of the headland where Thor had come ashore, and that's where he started the district assembly.[6] This place was so holy that he wouldn't let anybody desecrate it either with bloodshed or with excrement; and for privy purposes they used a special rock in the sea which they called Dritsker.[7]

By now, Thorolf was running his farm in fine style and had a good number of men with him. At that time there was plenty of food to be had both from the islands and from the sea.[8]

---

4. Lit. "Holy Mountain". There are several other Helga Fells in Iceland The name seems to reflect pre-Christian veneration.

5. See below, p. 51; and cp. *Njal's Saga*, tr. M. Magnusson & H. Pálsson, Penguin Classics, Harmondsworth 1960, p. 68: "Some fishermen at Kaldbak thought they had seen Svan being warmly welcomed into the innermost depths of Kaldbakshorn Mountain."

6. Before the Althing was instituted for the whole of Iceland in 930, there seem to have been two local assemblies: the Thor's Ness Assembly (mentioned here), and the Kjalar Ness Assembly, which was founded by Thorstein Ingolfsson, son of Iceland's first settler.   7. Lit. "Dirt Skerry".

8. The sea yielded fish, whales, and seals; the islands sea-fowl and eggs.

CHAPTER 5

In the Hebrides

NOW WE COME BACK to Bjorn Ketilsson, who had sailed west across the North Sea after his parting from Thorolf Mostur-Beard, which we have already described. By the time that he reached the Hebrides, his father Ketil had died, but he met his brother Helgi and their sisters, and they invited him to share in their prosperity. Bjorn discovered that they'd changed their beliefs and thought it very weak-minded of them to have renounced the old faith of their forefathers; so he didn't take at all kindly to them and wouldn't make his home there, though he did spend the winter with his sister Aud and her son Thorstein. When the family realised that Bjorn wasn't going to pay any attention to them, they started calling him Bjorn the Easterner, and thought less of him for having refused to settle there.

CHAPTER 6

Bjorn goes to Iceland

BJORN STAYED TWO YEARS in the Hebrides before getting ready for his voyage to Iceland, and when he left, Hallstein Thorolfsson went with him. They landed in Breida Fjord. With Thorolf's approval Bjorn took possession of land between the Staf River and Hraun Fjord, and built his farm at Borgarholt in Bjorn's Haven. People considered him a very brave man indeed. Hallstein Thorolfsson thought it a slur on his manhood that he should be granted land by his own father, so he crossed over to the other side of Breida Fjord, staked his own claim there, and settled at Hallstein's Ness.

Some years later Aud the Deep-Minded went to Iceland, where she spent her first winter with her brother Bjorn. Then she took possession of the whole of the Dales between Skrauma River and Dogurdar River, and made her home at Hvamm.[1] By this time all the districts round Breida Fjord had been fully settled, but it is unnecessary to mention here the settlements of people who don't come into our story.

CHAPTER 7

Other settlers

A MAN CALLED GEIRROD TOOK POSSESSION of land between Thor's River and Langdale, and made his home at Eyr. Ulfar the Champion came to Iceland with Geirrod, who granted him land round Ulfar's Fell, and along with them came Finngeir, son of Thorstein Ondur, who settled at Alftafjord. He was the father of Thorstein, father of Thorbrand of Alftafjord.

A man called Vestar, son of Thorolf Bladderbald, came to Iceland with his old father and took possession of land west of Urthvalar Fjord. He made his home at Ondurda Eyr, and his son Asgeir farmed there afterwards.

Bjorn the Easterner was the first of these settlers to die, and a

---

1. Aud's settlement is described in some detail in *Laxdæla Saga*, tr. Magnusson & Pálsson, pp. 53–5.

43

burial mound was raised over him at Borgarlæk. Two sons survived him, one of them Kjallak the Old, who inherited the farm at Bjorn's Haven after his father's death. His wife was Astrid, daughter of Hrolf the Chieftain and sister to Steinolf the Short. Kjallak and Astrid had three children: Thorgrim the Priest was their only son; and their daughters were Gerd, who married Thormod the Priest, son of Odd Rakki; and Helga, who became the wife of Asgeir of Eyr. A great many people are descended from Kjallak's children; and they are called the Kjalleklings.

Bjorn's other son was called Ottar. He married a woman called Gro, daughter of Geirleif and sister to Oddleif of Barda Strand; and their children were Helgi, father of Osvif the Wise,[1] Bjorn, father of Vigfus of Drapuhlid, and Vilgeir.

In his old age Thorolf Mostur-Beard married a woman called Unn, according to some people the daughter of Thorstein the Red, though Ari Thorgilsson the Learned doesn't include her among Thorstein's children.[2] Thorolf and Unn had a son called Stein. Thorolf dedicated the boy to his friend Thor and gave him the name Thorstein. He was a very promising lad, even at an early age.

Hallstein Thorolfsson married Osk, Thorstein the Red's daughter, and they had a son called Thorstein. Thorolf Mostur-Beard brought him up and nicknamed him Thorstein Surt. His own son he called Thorstein the Cod-Biter.

---

1. This Osvif was the father of Gudrun, the principal heroine of *Laxdæla Saga*, who is mentioned below, Chs. 56 and 64.
2. It is not known to which source this refers. For Ari, see *Laxdæla Saga*, tr. Magnusson & Pálsson, p. 51[3].

CHAPTER 8

Thorolf Twist-Foot

ABOUT THIS TIME GEIRRID, sister of Geirrod of Eyr, came to Iceland, and Geirrod granted her land at Borgardale, west of Alfta Fjord. She built a hall right across the road, so that every traveller had to ride through it. In the hall stood a table, always laden with food, and all were welcome to share it. Because of this people thought her a very remarkable woman indeed.

Geirrid had been married to Bjorn, son of Bolverk Blind-Snout, and they had a son called Thorolf, a great viking. He came out to Iceland some years after his mother and spent his first winter there with her. Thorolf thought that the lands which his mother had taken were not nearly wide enough, so he challenged Ulfar the Champion to single combat for the lands he owned, Ulfar being old and childless. Ulfar chose to die rather than let himself be bullied by Thorolf, and they fought a duel at Alftafjord. Ulfar was killed and Thorolf wounded in the leg, so he walked with a limp for the rest of his life and got the nickname Twist-Foot. Thorolf took over the land that had once belonged to Ulfar and set up house at Hvamm in Thorsardale. He was a very hard man.

Thorolf Twist-Foot sold some land to two freedmen who had belonged to Thorbrand of Alftafjord: Ulfar's Fell to one called Ulfar, and Orlygsstad to one called Orlyg; and that's where they lived for a long time afterwards.

Thorolf had three children, one of them a son, Arnkel. Thorolf's daughter Gunnfrid married Thorbeinir of Thorbeinisstad which stands on Vatnshals east of Drapuhlid. Their sons were Sigmund and Thorgils, and they also had a daughter, Thorgerd,

45

who married Vigfus of Drapuhlid. Thorolf Twist-Foot's second daughter was called Geirrid. She married Thorolf, son of Hrolf Holkinrazi, and they lived at Mavahlid. Their children were Thorarin the Black and Gudny.

CHAPTER 9

Desecration

WHEN THOROLF MOSTUR-BEARD DIED at Hofstad, Thorstein the Cod-Biter inherited his father's farm, and married Thora, Olaf's Daughter, the sister of Thord Gellir, who was at that time living at Hvamm.[1] A burial mound was raised over Thorolf at Haugsnes west of Hofstad.

By this time the Kjalleklings had grown so puffed up with arrogance they thought themselves better than anyone else in the settlements. Bjorn the Easterner had such a vast number of kinsmen there wasn't another family in Breidafjord to compare with his. At that time their kinsman Children-Kjallak was living at a farm in Medalfell Strand, now called Kjallaksstad. He had a good many sons, very able men who supported all their kinsmen on the south side of the bay at public meetings and other assemblies.

One spring at the Thor's Ness Assembly, Thorgrim Kjallaksson and his brother-in-law Asgeir of Eyr declared publicly that they weren't going to put up any longer with the Thorsnessings' pride, and meant to ease themselves there on the grass just as they would

---

1. Thord Gellir was one of the leading chieftains in 10th-cent. Iceland. He figures in *Laxdæla Saga*, *Hen-Thorir's Saga*, and below in Ch. 10.

at any other meeting, even though the Thorsnessings were so full of their own importance that they thought their land more sacred than any other in Breidafjord. The Kjalleklings let it be known that they weren't planning to waste any more shoe-leather on trips to an off-shore skerry whenever they felt the demands of nature. Thorstein the Cod-Biter heard about it. He had no intention of letting them desecrate the field his father Thorolf held sacred above all his land, so he gathered all his friends around him with the idea of barring the Kjalleklings from the Assembly ground by force should they attempt to desecrate it. These were men who backed Thorstein: Thorgeir the Bent, son of Geirrod of Eyr, Thorfinn of Alftafjord, his son Thorbrand, and Thorolf Twist-Foot; and plenty more friends and followers besides.

That evening, after the Kjalleklings had eaten, they took their weapons and went out to the headland. As soon as Thorstein and his men saw them turning off from the path to the skerry, they ran for their weapons and raced after them shouting abuse. The Kjalleklings saw them coming, and closed up ready to defend themselves, but the Thorsnessings went for them so fiercely that the Kjalleklings were forced to back down on to the beach. There they turned to face their attackers, and the fighting began in real earnest. There weren't as many of the Kjalleklings, but they had all the best fighters.

At this point the men of Skoga Strand, Thorgest the Old and Aslak of Langdale, realised what was happening and hurried over to intervene, but both parties were so bitter that there was no separating them until the mediators threatened to join the first side which listened to them. After that the two sides drew apart, on the understanding that the Kjalleklings were not to go back to the Assembly ground. This meant that they had to board their ship and leave the meeting. There had been deaths on both sides, particularly the Kjalleklings', and a good many wounded. It was impossible to arrange peace-terms, as neither side was willing to offer any, and each kept threatening to set on the other at the first opportunity. The spot where they'd fought and where the Thorsnessings had taken their stand was soaked with blood.

CHAPTER 10

Terms of settlement

AFTER THE FIGHT each side kept a standing force, and as feelings were running high between them, friends on both sides decided to send for Thord Gellir, who was at that time the leading chieftain in Breidafjord. He was a kinsman of the Kjalleklings, but was also closely related by marriage to Thorstein, so he seemed the most likely man to make peace between them. As soon as Thord got word, he set off with a number of men and tried to bring about a settlement, only to find how bitter their disagreement was. All the same, he managed to persuade them to accept a truce and a peace-meeting. As things turned out, it was agreed that Thord should arbitrate between them. The Kjalleklings stipulated that never again would they go out to Dritsker to ease themselves, while Thorstein demanded that no Kjalleklings should ever again be allowed to defile the Assembly Ground. The Kjalleklings insisted that those of Thorstein's men lost in the fighting had been killed lawfully, since they themselves had attacked with intent to kill. The Thorsnessings, on the other hand, claimed that because of the outrage committed by the others at a hallowed assembly, it was

48

perfectly lawful for anyone to kill the Kjalleklings. In spite of these awkward stipulations, Thord agreed to arbitrate rather than see the two sides part on bad terms again.

The first of Thord's decisions was that each side should keep the advantage gained. No compensation was to be paid for the killings and woundings on Thor's Ness. The field, he said, had been defiled by the spilling of blood in enmity, so the ground there was now no holier than any other. He said that those who were the first to attack and shed blood should be held responsible, as they were the ones who broke the peace, and that no assemblies should take place there in future. To ensure their friendship and reconciliation, Thord declared that from then on Thorgrim Kjallaksson was to bear half the cost of maintaining the temple, and that he and Thorstein were to share the temple dues and the support of the farmers equally between them. Thorgrim was also to back Thorstein in all his law-suits and safeguard the sanctity of whatever place Thorstein might choose for the new Assembly. One part of the agreement was that Thord Gellir gave his kinswoman Thorhild, daughter of his neighbour Thorkel Meinakur, in marriage to Thorgrim Kjallaksson, who from then on was known as Thorgrim the Priest.

This was when they moved the Assembly to the east side of the headland, where it is still held. And when Thord Gellir instituted the Quarter Courts,[1] he decided that the Court for the West

---

1. According to Ari Thorgilsson (*Book of Icelanders*, Ch. 5), it was at the suggestion of Thord Gellir that Iceland was divided into four Quarters for judicial purposes. The Quarter Courts dealt with law-suits between litigants from different local assemblies, but belonging to the same Quarter. See *Njal's Saga*, tr. Magnusson & Pálsson, pp. 54, 298–300.

Quarter – that is for all the people in the West Fjords – should meet there, too. The circle where the court used to sentence people to be sacrificed can still be seen, with Thor's Stone inside it, on which the victims' backs were broken; and you can still see the blood on the stone.[2]

Though this assembly place was held very sacred indeed, people were not forbidden to ease themselves there.

CHAPTER II

Thorstein the Cod-Biter dies

THORSTEIN THE COD-BITER RAN HIS FARM in fine style, and used to have thirty free men working for him. He was a generous provider and often went out fishing. Thorstein was the first to establish the farm at Helgafell; and when he moved house there, his temple made it a place of the very greatest importance. He took great pains over the building of another farm on the headland near the place where the Assembly had been held. This he gave to his kinsman Thorstein Surt, who lived there afterwards and had a reputation for exceptional shrewdness.

Thorstein the Cod-Biter had a son called Bork the Stout; then in the summer when Thorstein was twenty-five years old, Thora gave birth to another son, who was sprinkled with water and given the name Grim. Thorstein dedicated this boy to Thor, calling him Thorgrim, and said he should become a temple priest.

---

2. This is one of the few references to human sacrifice in pagan Iceland.

That same autumn Thorstein went to Hoskuld Island to fish. One evening in the autumn, as Thorstein's shepherd was tending sheep north of Helga Fell, he saw the whole north side of the mountain opened up, with great fires burning inside it, and the noise of feasting and clamour over the ale-horns. As he strained to catch particular words, he was able to make out that Thorstein the Cod-Biter and his crew were being welcomed into the mountain, and that Thorstein, was being invited to sit in the place of honour opposite his father.

That evening the shepherd told Thorstein's wife Thora about this vision. She was deeply disturbed by it and said it could be a foreboding of something very serious. In the morning some men brought news from Hoskuld Island that Thorstein the Cod-Biter had been drowned on a fishing trip. It was considered a terrible loss.

Thora kept the farm and took on an overseer called Hallvard to help her to run it. She had a son by him, called Mar.

CHAPTER 12

A new generation

THE SONS OF THORSTEIN THE COD-BITER GREW UP with their mother, both promising men, though Thorgrim outstripped his brother in every way. As soon as he was old enough, he became a temple priest. Thorgrim married Thordis, Sur's Daughter, in Dyrafjord and went to live there in the west with his brothers-in-law, Gisli and Thorkel. Thorgrim killed Vestein Vesteinsson at an autumn feast at Haukadale, and the following autumn when he was twenty-five years old, the very age his father had been when he was drowned, Thorgrim's brother-in-law Gisli killed him at an autumn feast at Sæbol. A few days later Thorgrim's widow Thordis gave birth to a boy, called Thorgrim after his father. A little later Thordis married her brother-in-law Bork the Stout and went to live with him at Helgafell,[1] but her son Thorgrim was sent to Alftafjord to be fostered by Thorbrand. Thorgrim was a very difficult child, so they called him Snerrir, and afterwards Snorri.[2]

Thorbrand of Alftafjord married Thurid, daughter of Thorfinn Sel-Thorisson from Raudamel, and these were their children: Thorleif Kimbi was the eldest, the second was Snorri, the third Thorodd, the fourth Thorfinn, and the fifth Thormod. Then there was a daughter as well, called Thorgerd. All of Thorbrand's sons were blood-brothers to Snorri Thorgrimsson.

At that time Arnkel, Thorolf Twist-Foot's son, was living at Bolstad near Vadilshofdi, a big strong fellow, clever at law and very shrewd. He was a great-hearted man and stood head and shoulders above all the other men in the district both in popularity and strength of character. Arnkel was a temple priest and had plenty of support.

As we've already said, Thorgrim Kjallaksson was living at Bjorn's Haven. He had three sons by his wife Thorhild. Brand, the eldest, was living at Kross Ness near Brimlar Head. The second,

---

1. This is a concise summary of the central plot of the tragic *Gisli's Saga*, which the author of *Eyrbyggja Saga* had evidently read. Vestein was Gisli's brother-in-law and blood-brother. According to *Gisli's Saga* it was Gisli's sister Thordis who, having discovered that he had killed her husband, urged her brother-in-law Bork the Stout to take revenge, after she had become his wife. 2. *Gisli's Saga* gives a similar account of the origin of Snorri's name. The words *snerrir* and *snorri* are cognates and have similar meanings: a turbulent, warlike man.

Arngrim, was a tall strong man, big-boned and ginger-haired, with a prominent nose. He'd gone bald at the temples while still a young man, his eye-brows came together, and his eyes were large and fine. He was a very arrogant man and unjust, which got him the name Styr.[3] Thorgrim's youngest son was Vermund, a tall man, slim and handsome, so people called him Vermund the Slender.

Asgeir of Eyr had a son called Thorlak who married Thurid, daughter of Audun Stoti of Hraunfjord, and their children were Steinthor, Bergthor, Thormod, Thord Blig, and Helga. Steinthor was the most promising of Thorlak's children. He was tall and strong, a skilled fighting-man of exceptional ability, but usually very quiet. Steinthor has been singled out as one of the three best fighters in Iceland, the other two being Helgi Droplaugarson and Vemund Fringe.[4] Thormod was shrewd and self-controlled, Thord Blig hot-tempered and outspoken. Bergthor was the youngest, but another man who showed great promise.

CHAPTER 13

Snorri travels to Norway

SNORRI THORGRIMSSON WAS FOURTEEN YEARS OLD when he went abroad with his blood-brothers, Thorleif Kimbi and Thorodd. His uncle Bork the Stout advanced him fifty ounces of silver for travelling expenses. They had a good passage, got to Norway in the autumn, and spent the winter in Rogaland, where

---

3. *Styr* means a "battle, skirmish", etc.   4. These heroes figure in *The Droplaugarsons' Saga* and the *Reykdœla Saga* respectively.

Snorri stayed with Erling Skjalgsson of Sola. Erling treated him well because of the old friendship between their ancestors, Horda-Kari and Thorolf Mostur-Beard.

The following summer they were late getting ready to sail back to Iceland, but after a difficult passage they made it into Horna Fjord just before winter. As they set out from the ship, these men of Breidafjord, there was a world of difference between the outfit of Snorri and that of Thorleif Kimbi. Thorleif had bought the best horse he could get, along with an elaborate, painted saddle. He carried an ornamented sword, a gold-inlaid spear, and a dark-blue, heavily gilded shield. All his clothes were of the very finest quality, and it was on this outfit that he'd spent most of his travelling money. Snorri, on the other hand, was wearing a black cloak and was riding a fine black mare. He'd got an old trough-shaped saddle, and his weapons were nothing much to look at. Thorodd's outfit came somewhere in between.

They rode through Sida and so by the usual route west to Borgarfjord, then across Vellir and at last got back home to Alftafjord. Next day Snorri rode over to Helgafell hoping to spend the winter there, but Bork was against it. Everybody kept laughing at Snorri because of his outfit, and Bork said he must have had bad luck with his money and lost the whole lot.

One day early in winter twelve men fully armed walked into the living-room at Helgafell. Their leader was Bork's kinsman, Eyjolf the Grey, Thord Gellir's son, who was living west at Otrardale in Arnarfjord. When people asked the news, they announced the killing of Gisli Sursson and those who'd fallen with him. This was good news to Bork, and he told Thordis and Snorri to give a hearty welcome to Eyjolf, the man who'd cleared away an ugly slur from the family's name.

Snorri had little to say about it, and Thordis said she knew of a welcome quite good enough for Gisli's killer. 'Let him eat gruel,' she said.

'It wasn't the food I had in mind,' said Bork.

He invited Eyjolf to take the seat of honour, then settled the others below him. The visitors laid their weapons on the floor. Bork was sitting next to Eyjolf on the far side, and after him, Snorri.

Thordis started carrying in the porridge-bowls with the spoons in them, and while she was serving Eyjolf she dropped one of the spoons. As she bent down to pick it up, she grabbed hold of Eyjolf's sword and made a quick thrust with it under the table. It caught Eyjolf in the thigh, but the pommel struck the table, checking the blow. All the same it was a nasty wound.

Bork shoved the table away from him and hit out at Thordis, but Snorri pushed Bork back away from her so hard that he fell over. Snorri put his arms round his mother and set her down beside him. He said her sorrow was great enough without her getting a beating too. Eyjolf and his men were on their feet and force had to be used to hold them back. The outcome of this was that Bork gave Eyjolf the right to decide how much compensation should be paid; and he awarded himself a large sum of money for the wound. After that he rode off. All this only served to increase the bad feeling between Bork and Snorri.

CHAPTER 14

Snorri wins Helgafell

AT THE DISTRICT ASSEMBLY the following summer Snorri demanded his inheritance from Bork. He told Snorri that he was quite ready to hand it over. 'However,' said Bork, 'I'm not dividing Helgafell. Something tells me we're not the kind of men to share the estate, so I'm going to buy you out and keep it for myself.'

'I'd call it more reasonable,' said Snorri, 'if you'd value the farm yourself and leave me to decide who's going to do the buying out.'

Bork thought this over and couldn't see how Snorri would ever have enough ready cash to pay for the farm. So he valued the estate at sixty ounces of silver and didn't include the islands, as he expected to be able to buy them up cheaply if Snorri got another farm. He also stipulated that the money should be handed over on the spot and that the buyer shouldn't be allowed to get himself into any man's debt in order to pay.

'Now, Snorri, it's up to you,' said Bork. 'You'd better make up your mind here and now.'

'Obviously, Bork,' said Snorri, 'you must be thinking me very short of money when you set such a low price on Helgafell. But I'm choosing to take my father's estate at this price, so give me your hand, and let's seal the bargain.'

'I'm not doing that till every penny's been paid,' said Bork.

Snorri turned to Thorbrand, his foster-father. 'Didn't I give you a money-purse last autumn?' he asked.

'Yes, you did,' said Thorbrand, and pulled out the purse from under his cloak. They counted the silver and paid out every penny for the estate. Even so, there were still sixty ounces of silver left in the purse.

Bork took the money and formally handed over the ownership of the estate to Snorri. 'Your purse turned out to be fuller than I'd expected, kinsman,' said Bork. 'Now I'd like us to forget the bad feeling that's grown up between us, and to show my good faith I'll give you a hand, and share in the running of the farm with you for the next year. After all, you've not much in the way of livestock.'

'You can keep your livestock,' said Snorri, 'and clear out of Helgafell.' And the way Snorri wanted it was how it had to be.

When Bork was about to leave, his wife Thordis came forward and declared in the presence of witnesses that she was divorcing him on the grounds that he'd struck her, and that she wasn't going to let herself be knocked about by him any longer. A division of their property was made, with Snorri acting for his mother, since he was her heir. Bork was forced to accept for himself what he'd meant for others, and also got very little for the islands.

After that Bork departed from Helgafell, and settled over in Medalfell Strand. He farmed first at Barkarstad between Orrahvall and Tongue, but later moved to Glerarwood; and there he lived till he was an old man.

CHAPTER 15

Snorri the Priest

SNORRI THORGRIMSSON STARTED FARMING at Helgafell, with his mother in charge of the household. Mar Hallvardsson, his uncle, moved over with plenty of livestock and became the farm's overseer. Snorri was soon running his farm in fine style, with plenty of men to follow him.

Snorri was a man of medium height and rather slight build, a handsome, regular-featured man with a fair complexion, flaxen hair, and a reddish beard. He was usually even-tempered, and it wasn't easy to tell whether he was pleased or not. He was a very shrewd man with remarkable foresight, a long memory, and a taste for vengeance. To his friends he was a sound adviser, but his enemies learned to fear the advice he gave. As Snorri was now in charge of the temple, he was called Snorri the Priest. He became a man of great power, and some people envied him bitterly, for there were plenty who thought themselves just as well-born, with a better claim to greatness, since they weren't lacking in followers and had proved their fighting spirit.

Bork the Stout and Thordis had a daughter called Thurid. She married Thorbjorn the Stout of Frodriver, son of Orm the Slender who had lived there before him and was the first man to settle at Frodriver, Thorbjorn had been married before to Thurid, daughter of Asbrand of Kamb in Breidavik and sister of Bjorn the Breidavik-Champion, who was later to play his part in the story. The sons of Thurid and Thorbjorn were Ketil the Champion, Gunnlaug, and Hallstein. Thorbjorn was powerfully built, and a hard man to everyone under him.

At this time Geirrid, Thorolf Twist-Foot's Daughter, and her son, Thorarin the Black, were living at Mavahlid. He was a big strong fellow, ugly to look at and taciturn, but normally very quiet, with the reputation of being a man of peace. Thorarin wasn't a wealthy man, but he had a valuable farm. He was so anxious not to get involved in things that his enemies said there was as much of the woman in him as the man. His wife was called Aud, and he had a sister, Gudny, who was married to Vermund the Slender.

A widow called Katla lived at Holt, west of Mavahlid. She was a fine-looking woman, but was not very well liked. She had a son called Odd, a big robust man, loud-mouthed, a born trouble-maker, and given to gossip and slander.

Thorbjorn the Stout's son, Gunnlaug, had a passion for know-ledge, and he often went over to Mavahlid to study witchcraft with Geirrid Thorolf's daughter, she being a woman who knew a thing or two. One day, when Gunnlaug was on his way over to Mavahlid, he called in at Holt and had a long talk with Katla. She asked him whether he was off to Mavahlid again 'to stroke the old hag up the belly.'

Gunnlaug said he wasn't going there for that. 'Are *you* so young, Katla,' he added, 'that you can afford to bring up Geirrid's age?'

'I wouldn't dream of making comparisons,' said Katla. 'But that's neither here nor there. You may not be able to think about anybody but Geirrid, but she's not the only woman with a few ideas in her head.'

Odd Katlason often went over with Gunnlaug to Mavahlid. Whenever they were late in coming back, Katla used to invite Gunnlaug to stay the night, but he always went straight home.

CHAPTER 16

Gunnlaug's mishap

ONE DAY EARLY IN THE FIRST WINTER that Snorri farmed at Helgafell, it happened that Gunnlaug Thorbjarnarson and

Odd Katlason went over to Mavahlid. Gunnlaug and Geirrid spent most of the day talking together, and late in the evening she said to him: 'I wish you wouldn't go back home tonight, there are too many sea-spirits about, and there's many a fair skin hides a foul mind. Anyway, you don't exactly have the look of a lucky man about you just now.'

'Nothing's going to happen to me,' said Gunnlaug, 'while there's two of us.'

'Odd won't be any use to you,' she said, 'you'll end up paying for your stubbornness.'

At that, Gunnlaug and Odd walked away from the farm, and over to Holt. Katla had gone to bed when they arrived there, and she asked Odd to invite Gunnlaug to stay the night. He said he'd already asked him, 'but he insists on going home.'

'Let him go, then,' she said, 'and face what's coming to him.'

Gunnlaug didn't come home that evening, and there was talk about making a search for him, but nothing came of it. During the night Thorbjorn looked outside and saw his son lying unconscious by the door. They carried him in and pulled off his clothes. He was scratched all over the shoulders and the flesh had been ripped to the bone. His injuries kept him in bed for the rest of the winter. There was a lot of talk about his illness, and Odd Katlason maintained that Geirrid must have bewitched him and ridden him for having taken such short leave of her that evening. Most people agreed that this was what must have happened.

In the spring at Summons Days,[1] Thorbjorn rode over to Mavahlid and served a summons on Geirrid for being a night-

1. The last days for serving a district-court summons were two weeks before the court convened.

witch and causing Gunnlaug bodily harm. The case was heard at the Thor's Ness Assembly. Snorri the Priest supported his brother-in-law Thorbjorn, and Arnkel the Priest acted on behalf of his sister Geirrid. A jury of twelve was appointed to try the case. Because of their kinship with plaintiff and defendant, neither Snorri nor Arnkel was qualified to testify, and Helgi the Priest of Hofgardar was chosen to give the verdict. (Helgi was the father of Bjorn, father of Gest, father of Poet-Ref.) Arnkel the Priest approached the court and swore an oath on the altar ring that Geirrid wasn't responsible for Gunnlaug's injuries, and Thorarin along with ten other men took the same oath. Then Helgi announced the jury's finding that there was no case to answer, and the charge preferred by Snorri and Thorbjorn was dismissed. The outcome was a great setback to them.

CHAPTER 17

Illugi the Black

AT THE SAME ASSEMBLY Thorgrim Kjallaksson and his sons quarrelled with Illugi the Black over the dowry of Illugi's wife Ingibjorg, Asbjorn's Daughter, which Tin-Forni had charge of. A fierce gale blew up during the Assembly, and no-one from Medalfell Strand could get through. It was a serious blow to Thorgrim that his kinsmen couldn't be there. Illugi had a hundred-and-twenty men with him, all good fighters, and pressed his claim hard. The Kjalleklings went to court with the idea of breaking it up. A mob began to form, but people forced their way in and

separated the two sides. In the end, after Illugi had argued the
matter out with him, Tin-Forni handed over the money.

This is what the poet Odd says in his eulogy on Illugi:

> *Crowds thronged west*
> *to the court at Thor's Ness,*
> *when the bold fortune-fighter*
> *won his wealth freely.*
> *Forni's gold passed,*
> *purse-packed, to the feeder*
> *of flesh-hungry ravens,*
> *hard-won peace followed rage.*

But later, when the gale had blown itself out and the Kjalleklings
were able to cross over from Medalfell Strand, Thorgrim Kjallaksson wouldn't honour the settlement and made an attack on Illugi.
When fighting began in real earnest, Snorri the Priest asked people
to help in calming things down, and managed to get a truce agreed
between them. The Kjalleklings lost three men killed in the battle,
Illugi four; and Styr Thorgrimsson himself killed two men there.
Odd has this to say about it in his eulogy on Illugi:

> *Pledged to keep peace,*
> *they dishonoured their promise,*
> *three doughty sword-flourishers*
> *struck down in the fight.*
> *Snorri the battle-seasoned*
> *settled the bitter business,*
> *won his well-earned praise*
> *wielding power firmly.*

Illugi thanked Snorri the Priest for all he'd done and asked him to accept a fee, but Snorri said he didn't want any payment for his help this time, though when Illugi invited him home, Snorri accepted. Illugi gave him some fine gifts, and for a time they stayed on friendly terms.

CHAPTER 18

Hostilities

IN THE SUMMER Thorgrim Kjallaksson died, and his son Vermund the Slender took over the farm at Bjorn's Haven. He was a shrewd man, and his advice was always sound. At that time Styr had been farming for a while nearby at Hraun, east of Bjorn's Haven. Styr, an intelligent and ruthless man, married Thorbjorg, Thorstein Sleet-Nose's Daughter, and their sons were Thorstein and Hall. They also had a daughter, Asdis, a fine woman, but rather proud-tempered. Styr lorded it over his neighbours and had plenty of men with him. He was involved in disputes with a good many people, as he'd killed a number of men without paying any compensation.

That summer a ship from overseas put in at Salteyrar Mouth. Some Norwegians owned a half-share in it; and their captain, Bjorn, went to stay the winter with Steinthor of Eyr. The other share belonged to a number of Hebrideans; and their captain, Alfgeir, went to Mavahlid and stayed with Thorarin the Black. Alfgeir had a companion called Nagli lodging there too, a man of Scottish origins, big and a very fast runner.

Thorarin kept a fine fighting stallion up in the mountains, and

Thorbjorn the Stout had a herd of stud-horses he left to graze on the mountain pasture, though he used to pick out some of them every autumn for slaughtering. That autumn it happened that Thorbjorn's horses couldn't be found anywhere, no matter how widely people searched. The weather was very bad that autumn.

At the beginning of winter Thorbjorn sent Odd Katlason over to Hraun south across the moor, where a man called Spa-Gils was living at the time. He had second sight and was very clever at investigating thefts and anything else which had to be sorted out. Odd asked him about Thorbjorn's horses: had they been stolen by foreigners, or by people from other districts, or by Thorbjorn's own neighbours?

'Tell Thorbjorn exactly what I'm going to tell you,' said Spa-Gils. 'I don't think his horses have strayed far from their usual pasture, and it's difficult to fix the blame on anybody. Better bear your losses than stir up a lot of trouble.'

When Odd came back to Frodriver, Thorbjorn and his men thought that the message from Spa-Gils hinted at the people of Mavahlid. Odd went on to suggest that Spa-Gils had meant something else, namely that the ones most likely to have stolen the horses would be those who were worst off for money and now had extra mouths to feed. It seemed to Thorbjorn that this could only refer to the men of Mavahlid.

Thorbjorn set off with eleven men. One of them was his son Hallbjorn, but his other son, Ketil the Champion, was abroad at the time. Another member of the party was Thorir Arnarson of Arnarhvall, Thorbjorn's neighbour and a great fighting-man. Odd Katlason came with him too. First they went over to Holt. Katla dressed her son Odd in a reddish-brown tunic which she'd just made. From there they rode on to Mavahlid. When they arrived,

Thorarin was standing outside the door with his servants. They'd seen the men coming up, and they greeted Thorbjorn, asking him the news.

'We've come here to look for the horses stolen from me in the autumn,' said Thorbjorn. 'I mean to search your premises.'

'Have you a proper warrant to search?' asked Thorarin. 'Have you appointed lawful witnesses to be present? What guarantees can you give for our safety while you're searching? Have you searched anywhere else?'

'I don't think there'll be any need to search elsewhere,' said Thorbjorn.

'If you're not prepared to go about it legally,' said Thorarin, 'I forbid you to search my premises.'

'Then we'll take it you're guilty,' said Thorbjorn, 'or you'd not have stopped us searching.'

'All right, do whatever you like,' said Thorarin.

Thorbjorn named six men to act as jury for the door-court,[1] and charged Thorarin with stealing the horses. Just then Geirrid came out of the door and saw what was going on.

'It's true what they say about you, Thorarin,' she said. 'You're more like a woman than a man, putting up the way you do with all Thorbjorn's insults. I can't think what I ever did to have a son like you.'

Then Alfgeir the ship's-captain said, 'We'll back you up all we can, whatever you decide to do.'

'I'm not standing around here any longer,' said Thorarin, and

---

1. Door-courts (*duradómar*) are not mentioned in the Icelandic laws; and it has been suggested that *Eyrbyggja Saga* may here preserve the memory of a judicial practice which went early out of use.

rushed forward with his men, meaning to break up the court. There were seven of them, and right away fighting broke out. Thorarin killed one of Thorbjorn's servants and Alfgeir another, then Thorarin lost one of his men as well, but not a weapon could bite Odd Katlason. Thorarin's wife Aud called on the women to separate the fighters, and they started throwing clothes on to their weapons. Then Thorarin and his men went back into the house, and Thorbjorn rode off with his party, threatening to raise the matter at the Thor's Ness Assembly. They rode over to the other side of the creek and dressed their wounds at a place called Korngard, beside a fenced-in haystack.

After the fight a human hand was found in the home meadow where they'd clashed at Mavahlid. Somebody showed the hand to Thorarin, and he saw it was a woman's, so he asked for Aud and was told she'd gone to bed. He went to see her and asked if she'd been hurt, but Aud told him not to fuss. Then he saw her hand had been cut off. Thorarin called out to his mother to come and dress the wound, then rushed out of the house with his men to go after Thorbjorn. As they came up to the haystack, they could hear Thorbjorn and his men talking away. Hallbjorn was speaking.

'Thorarin cleared himself of that slur on his manhood today,' he said.

'He fought like a real man,' said Thorbjorn. 'But then, most people are brave if they're driven into a corner, even if they're usually quite different.'

'Thorarin may be a brave man,' said Odd, 'but people won't think it very clever of him to have chopped off his wife's hand.'

'Is that true?' asked Thorbjorn.

'True as daylight,' said Odd.

They all began jumping about, jeering, and laughing, and just

at that moment Thorarin and his men came up with them. Nagli
was the first to get close, but when he saw them brandishing their
weapons, he lost his nerve and began racing up the hillside, scared
out of his wits. Thorarin made for Thorbjorn and with a sword-cut
split his head right down to the jaw. Then Thorir Arnarson and
two others set upon Thorarin, Hallstein and a companion tackled
Alfgeir, and Odd went with another man against one of Alfgeir's
shipmates. Three of Thorbjorn's men made a ferocious onset on
two of Thorarin's. Then Thorarin sliced through Thorir's leg at
the thick of the calf and killed both his men. Hallstein was cut
down by Alfgeir and mortally wounded. As soon as Thorarin was
free, Odd Katlason took to his heels, and two others ran off after
him. Odd was unharmed; no weapon could bite into his tunic. The
rest of Thorbjorn's men lay behind on the battlefield, and both of
Thorarin's servants were dead.

Thorarin and his men took Thorbjorn's horses and rode home.
On their way back they could see Nagli running along high up on
the hillside, and by the time they reached the home meadow,
Nagli had gone past the farmstead and was heading straight for
Buland Head. There he met two of Thorarin's slaves chasing sheep
away from the edge of the cliff. He told them about the fighting
and the odds, and said he knew for certain that Thorarin and all
his men must be dead by now. Just as he was telling them this,
they saw the men riding over the meadow. Thorarin and his
companions badly wanted to rescue Nagli and make sure he didn't
jump over the cliff or dive into the sea, so they spurred their horses
and raced towards him. When Nagli and the slaves saw the men
riding so hard, they thought it must be Thorbjorn and his companions, so they set off running towards the cliff and went on till
they got to a place now called Slaves' Scree. That's where Thorarin

and his men caught up with Nagli, who was now exhausted: but the slaves jumped off the cliff and were killed, just as you'd expect. It's so high, no living creature that falls down from there could possibly survive.

Then Thorarin and his men went home. Geirrid met them at the door and asked what had happened. Thorarin replied with a verse:

> *'In the court of weapons*
> *against charges of cowardice*
> *I've defended my honour,*
> *fought men to feed eagles.*
> *My sword bears witness*
> *it was put to the war-test:*
> *I don't care to boast,*
> *killing's not my business.'*

'Are you telling me Thorbjorn's been killed?' asked Geirrid. This was Thorarin's answer:

> *'My hard sharp edge*
> *aimed below the helmet;*
> *warm blood flowed reeking*
> *from the fierce warrior,*
> *in even streams sluiced*
> *down each side from the ears*
> *soaking the word-dry mouth.*
> *My stroke the more deadly!'*

'My words gave you an edge, then,' said she. 'Come in and let's see to your wounds.' And that's what they did.

Now we go back to Odd Katlason, who went on his way to Frodriver and told people the news. Thurid collected men to fetch the dead and wounded. Thorbjorn was laid in a burial mound, but his son Hallstein got better. So did Thorir of Arnarhvall, though he walked with a wooden leg for the rest of his life, and that got him the nickname Wood-Leg. He married Thorgrima Witch-Face, and their sons were Orn and Val, both sturdy fellows.

CHAPTER 19

After the fight

THORARIN SPENT THE NIGHT at home in Mavahlid, and next morning Aud asked him what he planned to do. 'I don't want to turn you out,' she said, 'but I'm afraid there are going to be more door-courts this winter. One thing I know for certain is that Snorri means to do something about the killing of his brother-in-law Thorbjorn.'

Thorarin said:

> *'The crafty law-breaker*
> *wouldn't bring me to outlawry,*
> *could I once catch the eye*
> *of one eager warrior:*
> *hungry ravens will feast*
> *on raw human flesh;*
> *I praise his valour,*
> *I trust Vermund's protection.'*

'Yes, that would be the sensible thing to do,' said Geirrid, 'to ask for the help of such kinsmen as Vermund. Or perhaps from my brother, Arnkel.'

'It's more than likely we'll be needing both before all this is over,' said Thorarin. 'But first I'll go and see what Vermund can do for us.'

That day all those who'd had a hand in the killings rode off east along the fjords and arrived at Bjorn's Haven in the evening. They walked straight into the living-room, where all the household was seated. Vermund greeted them; and, clearing the high-seat at once, he told Thorarin and his men to sit down. When they'd done so, Vermund asked the news. Thorarin said:

> *'Hear the truth, give*
> *your ear to my tale,*
> *in this troubled age*
> *of angry turmoil:*
> *the war-trained shield-bearers*
> *shook their spears at me;*
> *blades in their hands,*
> *I saw them, bloodstained.'*

'Can you tell me any more about it, kinsman?' asked Vermund. Thorarin went on:

> *'Angry came the warriors,*
> *so we killed them,*
> *my sword flashed against*
> *shield-bearing foes;*

we struck and left them
little to choose from;
yet I favoured peace,
till they forced my hand.'

Gudny, his sister, took the floor and asked, 'Have you cleared
your name of the charge of cowardice they were making against
you?' Thorarin said:

'*Slander drove me*
to defend my good name.
Ravens feasted then,
fattened by the spear's lust:
restless, the blade
rang, battering my helm;
blood-tides surged
like surf about me.'

'It seems to me you didn't waste any time before taking them
on,' said Vermund. Thorarin replied:

'*Steel-piercing shafts,*
screaming grim battle-songs,
swooped at my helm
and gold-rimmed shield:
my glittering screen
stained crimson with gore-paint,
the war-plain soaked
red with the blood-storm.'

'Did they find out for certain whether you're a man or a woman?'
asked Vermund. Thorarin said:

> *'My name's cleared now*
> *of the charge of cowardice;*
> *my challenger's dead,*
> *struck down by my weapons.*
> *Let Snorri whisper*
> *sweet words to his concubine;*
> *I've watched the ravens*
> *rip up the corpses.'*

After that Thorarin gave an account of what had happened.
Vermund asked: 'Why did you go after them? Didn't you think
enough had been done already?' Thorarin said:

> *'Soon they'll start accusing me*
> *of seeking to kill men:*
> *gone the good years*
> *when I used to go sailing.*
> *Traitors, cowards, they called out*
> *that I'd cut my own wife's arm,*
> *slandered me, jeered at me.*
> *Justice was all I sought!'*

'You've certainly got the excuse that you couldn't stand their
mockery,' said Vermund. 'And by the way, how did the foreigners
get on?' Thorarin replied:

'Scant food gave Nagli to gorge
the flesh-greedy ravens;
the cringing warrior fled
moaning up the mountain.
But helm-wearing Alfgeir
was eager for the war-game,
the warrior at play
with steel-polished weapons.'

'So Nagli didn't make much of an impression, then?' said Vermund. Thorarin went on:

'The shield-bearer took off
in tears from the battle-field;
fearing for his headpiece,
he flew from grim danger:
but all he dared
was to dive in the ocean,
to drown the sheer fright
of his faltering heart.'

After Thorarin had spent the night at Bjorn's Haven, Vermund had a word with him. 'You'll probably think me rather mean and not very keen to help you, kinsman,' he said, 'but I don't think I'm strong enough to offer you shelter unless there are other people who are ready to share in these troubles. So we'd better ride over to Bolstad today and see your kinsman Arnkel, to find out what help he's willing to give. I know Snorri the Priest won't be easy to deal with in this lawsuit.'

'I leave it all to you,' said Thorarin. While they were on their way, he made this verse:

> *Now our minds turn*
> *to the happy times*
> *before these hands dealt*
> *Thorbjorn's death-stroke.*
> *I'll be running soon*
> *from the rage of the proud one;*
> *how I hate the clash*
> *of the crimson shield-wall!*

This was meant as a hint to Snorri the Priest. So Vermund and Thorarin rode on their way till they came to Bolstad. Arnkel gave them a good welcome and asked the news. Thorarin said:

> *'The fight back home fills me*
> *with fear and horror,*
> *when fiery steel blades*
> *stripped life from flesh and bone;*
> *flashing spears bit*
> *our full-moon shields,*
> *sharp-edged brands*
> *battered our armour.'*

Arnkel asked Thorarin to tell him more about the matters he'd spoken of, and when he'd explained what had happened, Arnkel said, 'You must have got into quite a rage, kinsman, you're normally so quiet.' Thorarin said:

19: AFTER THE FIGHT

'People would call me
a man of peace,
for I've tried to hold back
the forces of hate:
but the ways of gentleness
can still guide us to war;
the gay life-loving widow
will soon learn my words.'

'Perhaps you're right,' said Arnkel. 'But, kinsman, I'd like you to stay with me till this whole affair's been settled one way or another. And, Vermund, I'd like you to keep giving your support, even though I've taken Thorarin under my wing.'

'It's my duty to help Thorarin all I can,' said Vermund; 'and even though you've taken charge of his case, my responsibility's no less than before.'

'I think it would be best,' said Arnkel, 'for us to stay here all together over the winter, close to Snorri the Priest.' And that's what they did.

So Arnkel had a lot of men staying with him that winter. Vermund spent some of the time home at Bjorn's Haven and some with Arnkel. Thorarin hadn't much to say for himself, and his mood never changed. Arnkel was a charming host, always good-tempered, and he didn't like others to be any less cheerful than himself. He often told Thorarin he should cheer up and not worry so much, and said he'd heard the widow of Frodriver was taking her loss remarkably well, 'so she'll think it a joke if you don't bear up like a man.' Thorarin replied:

'The fair dancing widow
won't boast at the beer-feast
that I'm afraid to see blood run.
I've watched ravens feed!
The birds of prey
will take their pleasure
while hard men breed
hatreds on the battlefield.'

One of Arnkel's servants said, 'You'll have to wait till after the Thor's Ness Assembly's over in the spring before you'll be able to decide how to get out of your troubles.' Thorarin replied:

'They tell me we'll suffer
setbacks in court,
so we must seek the counsel
of mighty chieftains:
but Arnkel will plead
an eloquent case,
sway judge and jury;
my faith stays firm.'

CHAPTER 20

Sorcerers put to death

GEIRRID OF MAVAHLID SENT WORD to Bolstad that she'd found out it was Odd Katlason who'd chopped off Aud's hand. She said she had this from Aud herself, and anyway Odd had been boasting about it to his friends. When Thorarin and Arnkel heard the story, they set out from home twelve strong and rode over to Mavahlid. They spent the night there and in the morning rode on to Holt. The people there saw them coming, but Odd was the only man at home just then. Katla was sitting in the living-room, spinning. She told Odd to sit down beside her. 'Keep quiet,' she said, 'and sit still.'

She told the women to stay in their usual seats. 'And keep quiet,' she said, 'I'll do all the talking for us.'

Arnkel and his men came up to the farmstead and went straight in. As they walked into the living-room, Katla greeted them and asked the news. Arnkel said he had none to speak of, and asked for Odd. Katla said he'd gone south to Breidavik. 'And if he were at home, he wouldn't try to avoid you,' she said. 'We've no doubt about your being men of principle.'

'That's as may be,' said Arnkel, 'but we're going to search the house.'

'Just as you wish,' said Katla, and told her housekeeper to carry a light for them and open the store-room. 'It's the only locked room in the house,' she added.

They could see that Katla was spinning yarn on her distaff. They searched all over the house but didn't find Odd, so off they went. When they'd gone a little way, Arnkel stopped in his tracks. 'Did Katla use her witchcraft to make fools of us, I wonder?' he asked. 'Could it be that the thing we thought was a distaff was really her son Odd?'

'That would be just like her,' said Thorarin, 'let's go back.' And that's what they did. When the people at Holt saw them coming back, Katla said to the women, 'You stay in the room where you are. Odd and I are going outside.'

As they left the room, she slipped into the vestibule beside the door and started combing and trimming Odd's hair. Arnkel and his men came rushing inside, and all they could see was Katla playing around with a goat. She seemed to be trimming its forelock and beard and combing its wool. Arnkel and his men went into the living-room but still couldn't see Odd anywhere, and Katla's distaff was lying on the bench. They made sure Odd couldn't have been hiding there, then walked out of the house and went away.

When they came to the spot where they'd turned back before, Arnkel said, 'Don't you think it could have been Odd masquerading as a goat?'

'Who knows?' said Thorarin. 'Let's turn back right away and get our hands on Katla.'

'We'll give it another try,' said Arnkel, 'and see what happens.' So once again they turned back.

When Katla saw them coming up, she told Odd to take a walk with her. They went outside over to the rubbish-heap, and she told him to lie down next to it. 'Stay here whatever happens,' she said.

Arnkel and his men came up to the farmstead and rushed into the living-room. Katla was sitting on the daïs, spinning. She greeted them and said they'd become quite regular callers, and Arnkel had to admit it. His companions grabbed the distaff and started chopping it up.

'Now that you've broken my distaff,' said Katla, 'you can tell your people back home tonight that your visit to Holt wasn't entirely wasted.'

Arnkel and his men searched for Odd inside and out and couldn't find a living creature except Katla's pet hog lying by the rubbish-dump, so they went away.

When they were halfway to Mavahlid, Geirrid came to meet

78

them with one of her servants and asked how they'd got on. Thorarin told her what had happened.

She said they hadn't made a proper search for Odd. 'I want you to turn back once again,' she said, 'and this time I'm coming with you, for there's no point in dealing gently with Katla.'

So they turned back. Geirrid was wearing a blue cloak. The people at Holt saw them coming, and Katla was told there were now fourteen of them, one in bright-coloured clothes.

'That must be Geirrid the witch,' said Katla, 'and this means that something more than sorcery's needed.'

She stood up on the daïs and lifted the cushions she'd been sitting on. There was a trapdoor in the floor with a hollow place underneath. She told Odd to get down into it, and then she arranged everything as it had been before. As she sat down, she told them a strange feeling had come over her.

Arnkel and his party came into the room, and this time there were no greetings. Geirrid threw off her cloak, went up to Katla, and pulled a sealskin bag over her head. Her companions tied the bag firmly round Katla's neck. Then Geirrid told the men to break open the floor, and there they found Odd and tied him up. After that mother and son were taken east to Buland Head, and Odd was hanged there. As he was kicking on the gallows, Arnkel said to him, 'It's your own mother who's brought you to this. One thing's sure, it's a wicked mother you've got!'

'Maybe he has got a wicked mother,' said Katla, 'but I never wanted him to come to this. I hope every one of you will go through agonies because of me – in fact I know you will. There's no point in denying it any longer, I'm the one who caused Gunnlaug's mishap, and all these troubles stemmed from me. As for you, Arnkel, since *your* mother's dead, she can't bring you bad luck, but I lay this curse on you, that before this is over you'll suffer more because of your father than Odd has suffered because of me. The time is coming when everyone will see what a scoundrel you've got for a father.'

Then they stoned Katla to death just below the cliffs. After that they went back to Mavahlid, stayed the night there, and rode back home the following day. The news of what had happened soon spread, but no-one had any misgivings about it. So another winter passed.

CHAPTER 21

Arnkel's advice

ONE DAY IN THE SPRING Arnkel sent for his kinsman, Thorarin, along with Vermund and Alfgeir, and asked them what kind of help they wanted most from him. Should all go together to the assembly and ask their friends for help? 'There seem to be two ways of looking at it,' he went on, 'if there's a settlement you'll have to pay out a great deal of money in compensation for those killed or wounded, though our presence in court may make matters worse, particularly if we put our case very strongly. The other course open to us is to do everything we can to help you get abroad with all your money, and chance what's to become of the farm if we can't sell it.'

This was the kind of help Alfgeir thought best, and anyway Thorarin said he couldn't afford to pay compensation for all the offences he had committed. Vermund said he wouldn't let Thorarin down, no matter whether he wanted Vermund to go abroad with him or support him against his enemies in Iceland. Thorarin decided to accept Arnkel's offer to help him go abroad. So they sent a message west to Eyr, telling Bjorn, the captain, to get their ship ready as soon as he could.

CHAPTER 22

Exile

NOW WE COME BACK to Snorri the Priest, who'd taken charge of the action over the killing of his brother-in-law Thorbjorn. He asked his sister Thurid to come and stay at Helgafell, as rumour had it that Bjorn Asbrandsson of Kamb was paying regular visits to Frodriver and carrying on with her. When Snorri heard that the ship was being made ready, he realised it must be Arnkel's plan not to pay any compensation for the killings, since there had not been any offer of a settlement.

All the same, things were quiet till Summons Days. Then Snorri gathered a force and rode eighty strong over to Alftafjord. It was the law in those days that the summons for manslaughter had to be made within earshot of the killers or wherever they lived, but neighbours were not cited as witnesses till the assembly was due.

When the men of Bolstad saw Snorri's party coming up, they began arguing whether or not to fight, as there was a good crowd of them. But Arnkel was against it. 'Snorri's going to have his legal rights,' he said, and told them not to do anything that wasn't necessary.

When Snorri got to Bolstad, nobody made any trouble. He summonsed Thorarin and all the others involved in the killings to

the Thor's Ness Assembly. Arnkel listened closely. Then Snorri
and his men rode off to Ulfarsfell, and after they'd gone, Thorarin
made this verse:

> *Not for desperate crimes*
> *do they deny justice*
> *to one who's endured*
> *the dark storm of war;*
> *my shield-bearing enemies*
> *would brand me an outlaw.*
> *Grant us the force, gods,*
> *to face those against us.*

Snorri the Priest rode across the ridge to Hrisar, over to
Drapuhlid, then next morning west by Svinavatn to Hraun Fjord,
and from there by the normal route west to Trollahals, without
breaking his journey till he came to the Salteyrar Mouth, where
some of his men laid hands on the Norwegian crew and the others
began burning the ship. When this was done, Snorri the Priest
and his men rode back home.

When Arnkel heard that Snorri had burnt the ship, he boarded
a boat with Vermund and several others and rowed north across
the fjord over to Dogurdar Ness, where a Norwegian ship was
beached. Arnkel and Vermund bought it, and Arnkel gave
Thorarin his share, but Vermund kept the other half. They sailed
the ship out to Dimun Island and fitted it out for the voyage.
Arnkel stayed with them till they were ready to put out, then went
with them as far as Ellida Island, where they parted the best of
friends. Thorarin and Vermund sailed out to sea, and Arnkel went

back to his farm. Everybody agreed that he'd been very generous with his help.

Snorri the Priest went to the Thor's Ness Assembly and pressed his charges. The outcome was that Thorarin and all those involved with him in the killings were sentenced to outlawry. After the Assembly Snorri confiscated all their property he could lay hands on, and that was the end of the law-suit.

CHAPTER 23

Insults

AS WE'VE ALREADY SAID, Vigfus, son of Bjorn Ottarsson, lived at Drapuhlid and married Thorgerd, Thorbeinir's Daughter. Vigfus was a good farmer, but a difficult man to get on with. He had a nephew called Bjorn staying with him, a loose-tongued, worthless sort of fellow.

In the autumn after the Mavahlid affair, Thorbjorn the Stout's herd of horses was found dead up in the mountains. His stallion had been driven from the pastures by Thorarin's and then the whole herd had been snowed under and killed.

That same autumn a crowd of people gathered at Tunga between the Lax Rivers south of Helga Fell to shed the sheep. Snorri sent some of his men there with his uncle Mar Hallvardsson in charge. Snorri had a shepherd called Helgi. Bjorn, Vigfus's nephew, was lying on top of the wall of the pen holding a shepherd's crook, while Helgi was sorting out the sheep. Bjorn asked him whose sheep he'd just taken, and when they looked at it, they saw it had Vigfus's earmarks.

'You're not very particular about the sheep you're picking up today,' said Bjorn.

'It's even riskier for you,' said Helgi, 'living so close to common pasture.'

'What could a thief like you mean by that?' said Bjorn. He jumped to his feet and lashed out at Helgi with the crook, knocking him senseless.

Mar saw what had happened, pulled out his sword, and lunged at Bjorn. The thrust caught him in the arm just below the shoulder, giving him a nasty wound. At that the sheep-sorters took sides, but some men stepped in and broke up the fighting, so for the present nothing happened.

Next morning Vigfus rode down to Helgafell and demanded compensation for the insult, but Snorri said he wasn't able to judge between the two incidents. Vigfus got into a temper, and they parted on chilly terms.

In the spring Vigfus raised a court action over the wounding and put the case before the Thor's Ness Assembly, but Snorri made a counter-charge against Bjorn. Bjorn was found guilty of unlawful assault on Helgi, and he got no compensation for the wound, even though he carried his arm in a sling after that.

CHAPTER 24

Eirik the Red

AT THIS ASSEMBLY Thorgest the Old and the sons of Thord Gellir brought an action against Eirik the Red for the killing of Thorgest's sons the autumn before, when Eirik went over to

Breidabolstad to claim his bench-boards. It was a well-attended Assembly. Each side had kept a large standing force.

During the Assembly Eirik got his ship ready at Eirik's Bay on Oxna Island. He got the backing of Thorbjorn Vifilsson, Killer-Styr, the sons of Thorbrand of Alftafjord and Eyjolf Æsuson of Svin Island, but of all his supporters Styr was the only one who attended the Assembly. He persuaded all the men he could to withdraw their support from Thorgest, and then he pleaded with Snorri the Priest not to join Thorgest in the attack on Eirik after the Assembly. In return he promised to back Snorri any time he had trouble on his hands. Snorri accepted the offer and took no part in the quarrel.

After the Assembly Thorgest and his men set out to the islands in a number of boats, but Eyjolf Æsuson hid Eirik's ship in Dimun Bay, and that's where Styr and Thorbjorn came to join Eirik. Eyjolf and Eirik did just as Arnkel had done and went with Eirik out beyond Ellida Island, each in his own boat.

It was on this voyage that Eirik the Red discovered Greenland. He stayed there for three years, and then went back to Iceland. The following year he set out to colonise Greenland, fourteen years before Christianity was adopted by law in Iceland.[1]

---

1. The events in this chapter, culminating in Eirik the Red's colonisation of Greenland in 985 or 986, are described in more detail in *Eirik's Saga* and *Grænlandinga Saga*. See *The Vinland Sagas*, tr. Magnusson & Pálsson.

CHAPTER 25

The Swedish berserks

NOW WE COME BACK to Vermund and Thorarin the Black. They made landfall in Norway north of Trondheim Fjord and sailed up to Trondheim. The ruler of Norway at the time was Earl Hakon Sigurdarson.[1] Vermund went to see him and became his retainer, but in the autumn Thorarin sailed west with Alfgeir to the British Isles and Vermund gave them his share in the ship. Now Thorarin is out of the story.

Earl Hakon was in residence at Lade that winter, and Vermund stayed with him there in great favour. The Earl knew that Vermund belonged to an important family in Iceland, and that was why he treated him so well.

With the Earl were two Swedish brothers called Halli and Leiknir. They were by far the biggest and strongest men in Norway, or anywhere else, at that time. They were berserks, and once they had worked themselves up, they were completely beside themselves, storming about like mad dogs and afraid of neither fire nor weapons. Most of the time they weren't too hard to get on with as long as they were left in peace, but once anybody gave them the slightest offence, they became extremely violent. King Eirik, the conqueror of Sweden,[2] had given them to the Earl and warned him to take great care of them. The King told him nothing less than the truth, that the berserks were grand men to have as allies, as long as their tempers remained under control.

In the spring when Vermund had been staying a winter with

---

1. Earl Hakon Sigurdarson was ruler of Norway 975–99.

2. King Eirik ruled Sweden from c.950 to c.993.

the Earl, he wanted to go back to Iceland and asked him for leave to sail. The Earl said he could go if he wished, but asked him to think about something first. 'Is there anything of mine you'd particularly like to have,' he said, 'a gift which would add to your splendour and do honour and credit to both of us?'

Vermund thought it over, wondering what he should ask for. Then it struck him how much it would strengthen his position in Iceland if he could have the berserks for followers, so he made up his mind to find out if the Earl would give him the berserks. Vermund had a good reason for wanting them. It seemed to him that his brother Styr was growing more than a match for him, for Styr kept bullying him, just as he bullied almost everyone else. With the berserks to back him up, Vermund did not think Styr would find it so easy to push him around.

So Vermund told the Earl he'd consider it an honour if he'd give him the berserks to serve him and guard him. 'It seems to me,' said the Earl, 'that you've asked for the one thing that's going to be no use to you, even if I grant it. I know you'll find the berserks rough and arrogant if you don't get on with them. As I see it, controlling those ruffians and keeping them in their place is going to be far too much for a mere farmer's son, even though they've been quiet enough in my service.'

Vermund said he was ready to risk it, if the Earl agreed to give them to him. The Earl told him to find out first from the berserks themselves whether they'd go with him, and Vermund did so. He asked if they'd be his men and come with him to Iceland, and in return he promised to treat them well and give them anything they wanted, should they ask for it. The berserks said they'd never thought of going to Iceland, for, from what they'd heard, there wasn't a chieftain there to suit them.

'But since you're so keen to take us with you to Iceland, Vermund,' they said, 'we want you to know this, that if ever you refuse to give us anything which we ask and you have the power to grant, we won't be at all pleased.'

Vermund said it would never come to that, and got their promise to come with him to Iceland, provided the Earl gave his approval. Vermund went to see the Earl and told him what had happened, and the Earl decided the berserks should go with him to Iceland, 'since you think it'll do so much for your prestige.' But he gave a warning that he'd consider it a personal affront if Vermund were to treat them badly once they became his men. Vermund said there was no reason to think it would ever come to that. Then he set off to Iceland with the berserks aboard. He had a good passage and got back home the same summer that Eirik the Red sailed to Greenland, as we've said.

Soon after Vermund came home, the berserk Halli said he wanted Vermund to find him a suitable wife, but Vermund didn't know of any respectable woman who wanted to be landed with a berserk for the rest of her life, so he kept putting him off. When Halli saw what was happening, he became rough and bad-tempered, and this led to a bitter quarrel between them. The berserks kept swaggering about threatening Vermund, and he began to regret ever having taken them in.

In the autumn Vermund gave a great feast and invited his brother Styr, Arnkel the Priest, and the men of Eyr. After the feast Vermund offered Arnkel the berserks and said they'd come in very useful, but Arnkel wouldn't accept the gift. Then Vermund asked Arnkel for advice about how to get out of his trouble, and Arnkel suggested giving the berserks to Styr. 'He's so arrogant and unjust,' said Arnkel, 'that he's most likely to be able to cope with them.'

So when Styr was ready to go, Vermund came up and spoke to him. 'Brother,' he said, 'I'd like to put an end to the coolness there's been between us since before I went abroad. We ought to remember our kinship and stay good friends. I'd like to give you these two warriors I brought from Norway, to serve you and guard you. With followers like them to back you up I can't think of anyone who'd have the strength to stand up to you.'

'I'd very much like us to be on friendlier terms, brother,' said Styr, 'but from what I've heard about these men you brought to Iceland, they'd be a liability rather than an asset, and won't bring anyone much luck. I'm certainly not having them in my house. I'm unpopular enough as it is, without their adding to my troubles.'

'What advice would you give me, then, brother, to get me out of this?' asked Vermund

'That's a different matter entirely,' said Styr. 'To help you out of your troubles is one thing, getting these men as a gift from you is quite another. I'm not having them on any account. Still, now we're friends again, I suppose there's no-one more duty-bound to help you out than I am.'

Yet, in spite of Styr's objections, Vermund persuaded him to take the berserks. The brothers parted the best of friends, and Styr went back home taking the berserks with him. At first they wouldn't go and said Vermund hadn't any right to sell them or give them away, but in the end they had to admit it would suit them better to serve Styr than Vermund.

To start with, the berserks and Styr got on well. They both went with him on his trip across the bay when he killed Thorbjorn Kjalki of Kjalkafjord. Thorbjorn had a bed-closet built with thick beams, but the berserks forced the joints apart, and they were able

to break into it without any trouble at all, though it was Styr
himself who killed Thorbjorn Kjalki.

CHAPTER 26
Attempt on Snorri's life

ONE DAY IN AUTUMN after the berserks had come to stay
with Styr, Vigfus of Drapuhlid set out with three slaves to
make charcoal at a place called Seljabrekkur. One of the slaves
was called Svart the Strong. As they were going through the wood,
Vigfus said, 'It's a sad thing, Svart, when a good strong fellow like
you isn't a free man. You must feel it badly.'

'I take it hard,' said Svart, 'but there's nothing I can do about
it.'

'What would you do for me if I gave you your freedom?' asked
Vigfus.

'Since I haven't got any money, I can't buy my freedom,' said
Svart, 'but if there's something I can do to get it, then I'm ready
for anything.'

'Go over to Helgafell and kill Snorri the Priest,' said Vigfus,
'and once you've done that, you can have your freedom and plenty
more besides.'

'I'll never manage it,' said Svart.

'I'll tell you how to go about it,' said Vigfus. 'I guarantee there
won't be any risk to your life.'

'Tell me more,' said Svart.

'Go over to Helgafell and into the loft above the main door.
Then pull up a plank or two from the floor so that you can push

your halberd through the gap, and when Snorri goes out to the privy, drive the halberd hard down into his back so that the blade goes right through his body. Then climb on to the roof, jump down from the wall, and get away under cover of darkness.'

With these instructions in mind Svart set off over to Helgafell. He broke a hole in the ceiling above the main door and scrambled into the loft. While all this was going on, Snorri and his men were sitting by the fire. In those days every farm had an outside privy. When Snorri and his men got up from the fire to go out, he was ahead of the rest, and by the time Svart made his thrust, Snorri was already through the door. Mar Hallvardsson came close on Snorri's heels, and it was he who took Svart's blow. The blade caught him in the shoulder and sliced him across the arm, but it wasn't a serious wound. Svart scrambled out on to the roof and jumped down from the wall, but slipped on the pavement. It was a nasty fall, and Snorri had him before he could get back on to his feet. Once they started questioning him, he not only told them everything that had happened between Vigfus and himself, but also where Vigfus was, making charcoal at Seljabrekkur.

When Mar's wound had been seen to, Snorri set out over to Drapuhlid with six men. As they were making their way up the hillside they could see the fire where Vigfus and his slaves were making the charcoal. They took them by surprise and put Vigfus to death, but spared his slaves. With that Snorri went home, and sent the slaves back to Drapuhlid to tell people the news. Next morning a burial mound was raised over Vigfus, and that same day his widow Thorgerd went over to Bolstad to tell her uncle Arnkel about it. She asked him to take action over the killing, but he wouldn't and said it was the business of the Kjalleklings, who were Vigfus's kinsmen. He suggested that Styr should be the one to raise the action, particularly since he was always meddling in everything.

Thormod Trefilsson made this verse about the killing of Vigfus:

> *Snorri the war-leader*
> *struck and felled*
> *his first victim*
> *when he laid Vigfus low,*
> *left his corpse*
> *for the greedy carrion-birds*
> *to gorge their fill*
> *on gobbets of flesh.*

CHAPTER 27

Thorgerd gets help

THORGERD WENT OVER to Hraun and asked Styr to take action over the killing of his kinsman Vigfus.

'Last spring, when Snorri the Priest kept out of our quarrel with the Thorgestlings,' said Styr, 'I promised him that I'd never act against him in a law-suit as long as there were plenty of others as deeply involved as myself. You'd better ask either my brother Vermund to take up the case, or some-one else in our family.'

So Thorgerd made a trip out to Bjorn's Haven and asked Vermund for help. She said it was really his business, 'because,' she said, 'Vigfus trusted you before any of his kinsmen.'

'I agree it's my duty to help you in the case,' said Vermund. 'I'm not going to shoulder my kinsmen's burden, but I'll help you all I can with advice and backing. First, I want you to go over to Eyr and see Steinthor, Vigfus's kinsman. He's always spoiling for a fight, and it's about time he tried his hand at a law-suit.'

'You're all putting me to a lot of trouble,' Thorgerd said, 'but I won't hang back if I can get results.'

Next she went over to Eyr to see Steinthor and asked him to take over the action for manslaughter.

'Why come to me for help?' asked Steinthor. 'I'm only a young man, and I've never taken part in a law-suit before. Vigfus had plenty of kinsmen closer to him than I am and a lot more pushing, so I can hardly be expected to take this case off their hands. But, of course, if my kinsmen decide to take action over the killing, I won't let them down.'

And that was all the answer Thorgerd could get out of him. So she travelled to the other side of the fjord to see Vermund, told him what had happened, and said it would be the end of her law-suit if he didn't take charge.

'There's still a good chance that action will be taken, which should be some consolation to you,' said Vermund. 'If you promise to follow my advice, I'll tell you what to do.'

'I'd do almost anything to help,' she said.

'All right,' said Vermund, 'go back and have your husband's body dug up, then take his head to Arnkel. Tell him this head wouldn't have left the action to others if Arnkel had needed it.'

Thorgerd said she couldn't see how that was going to help. As far as she could tell, everybody seemed only too keen to add to her trouble and misery. 'But I'll do as you suggest,' she said. 'I can only hope it'll make my enemies suffer.'

So she went back home and did everything as she'd been told. When she came to Bolstad, she told Arnkel that her husband's kinsmen wanted him to take charge of the manslaughter action over Vigfus and that they'd promised to back him up. Arnkel said he'd already told her what he thought of the case, but just then she pulled the head from under her cloak.

'Here's a head,' she said, 'that would never have shirked action if you'd been killed and its help had been needed.'

Arnkel was horrified and pushed her away.

'Clear out of here,' he said, 'and tell Vigfus's kinsmen they'd better be just as firm in backing me against Snorri the Priest as I'll be in pressing charges. I don't know how this case will turn out, though it's certain I'll be the very last to give up. It's obviously Vermund who gave you this advice, but if I and my in-laws are fighting the same battle, it won't be me he'll have to goad into action.'

With that Thorgerd went back home.

The winter passed and in the spring Arnkel started a manslaughter action against all those who had taken part in the attack on Vigfus, with the exception of Snorri the Priest. But Snorri brought a counter-action for attempted manslaughter on his own behalf, and another action for the wounding of Mar, claiming that Vigfus had been lawfully killed. Both sides came to the Thor's Ness Assembly with a large following, but all the Kjalleklings supported Arnkel, and they had the biggest force. Arnkel pleaded the case forcefully, but when judgment was about to be passed, peace-makers intervened, and thanks to their plea the whole issue was referred to arbitration. Snorri agreed to accept the verdict of the arbitrators. For the killing of Vigfus he was made to pay a large fine, and Mar was to stay abroad for three years. Snorri paid his fine on the spot, and when the Assembly broke up, every law-suit had been settled peacefully.

CHAPTER 28

The end of the berserks

NOW WE TAKE UP THE STORY where we left off before. The berserks hadn't been long in Styr's service, when Halli began fancying Styr's daughter Asdis. She was a splendid-looking young woman, but very proud and self-assured. When Styr found out they'd been talking together, he told Halli not to bring shame and disgrace on him by trying to seduce his daughter.

'I've said nothing to your daughter for you to be ashamed of,' said Halli. 'I'm not just doing it to make trouble, and I might as well tell you straight out that I'm so much in love with her I can't put her out of my mind. I want you and me to be close friends. Let me marry your daughter Asdis, and in return I'll give you my word and swear to be your loyal friend. The support you'll get from my brother Leiknir and me will be the staunchest ever given by any two men in the whole of Iceland. Our backing will do more to raise your status here than if you were to marry off your daughter to the greatest farmer in Breidafjord, and that should make up for my lack of money. But if you decide to turn me down, it'll be the end of our friendship, and then each of us will just have to take what's coming to him. In any case there's not much you can do to stop me talking with Asdis.'

When Halli had spoken his piece, Styr stayed very quiet, not knowing what to say. After a while he said, 'Is this a serious proposal, or are you just playing about and trying to start an argument?'

'Whatever your answer,' said Halli, 'get one thing clear, I'm not doing this for a joke. Our whole friendship depends on what you have to say about it.'

'Before I can give you an answer, I'll have to ask my friends about it,' said Styr.

'I give you three days to talk it over with anyone you like,' said Halli, 'but you're not putting me off any longer than that, for I'm not the kind of suitor who cares to be kept waiting.'

With that they parted. Next morning Styr rode over to Helgafell and saw Snorri, who asked him to stay. Styr said he only wanted to have a word and then ride back home. Snorri asked if it was something serious he wanted to discuss.

'I'd call it that,' said Styr.

'Then we'd better go to the top of Helga Fell,' said Snorri. 'Plans made there have never been known to fail.'

'It's up to you,' said Styr.

They went to the top of the hill and sat there talking together till evening, but nobody knew what they were talking about. After that Styr rode back home.

Next morning Styr took Halli aside, and Halli asked what he was doing about the proposal.

'Everybody thinks you're far too badly off,' said Styr. 'Are you willing to make up for your poverty?'

'I'll do whatever I can,' said Halli, 'but it can't be to lay out money, as I haven't got any.'

'I can see you'd be offended if I didn't let you marry my daughter,' said Styr, 'so I'm going to do the same as people used to do in the old days. Before you win her hand, I'll set you a few difficult tasks.'

'What have you got in mind?' asked Halli.

'Clear a path right across the lava field, all the way to Bjorn's Haven,' said Styr, 'then set up a dyke across the lava to mark the boundary-line between the two farms, and finally build a sheep-shed on my side of the dyke. Once you've managed all that, you can have my daughter as your wife.'

'I'm not used to hard work,' said Halli, 'but I'll gladly agree to anything that helps smooth the path to marriage.'

So Styr said they'd arrange terms about it.

The berserks set to work clearing the path, and it was a really vast undertaking. Next they set up the dyke – you can still see traces of it. When they'd finished the dyke, they started on the sheep-shed; and while they were working away, Styr had a bath-house built on his farm at Hraun. It was partly below ground level, and immediately above the fireplace, was a skylight for pouring water through from the outside. This bath-house was a really hot one.

When the two berserks had nearly finished their allotted tasks and on the very last day were busy at the sheep-shed, Styr's daughter Asdis went out for a walk near the farmhouse wearing her finest clothes and came quite close to them. Halli and his brother spoke to her, but she took no notice. Then Halli made this verse:

> '*Tell me, my gold-adorned*
> *elegant good friend,*
> *where are your graceful*
> *steps guiding you now?*
> *This whole winter season*
> *I've never seen you*
> *go for a stroll*
> *so finely attired.*'

Leiknir said:

> '*No lady can ever*
> *have carried so loftily*
> *her gold-coiffed head*
> *as this elegant girl.*
> *What deep mystery*
> *does your display mask?*
> *In your sweet, smooth voice*
> *speak your secret.*'

But she walked away from them. That evening the berserks came home, completely worn out. This is what happens to those who go berserk. Once the rage leaves them, they seem to lose all their strength. Styr came out to welcome them and thanked them for what they'd done. He invited them to take a bath and after that a rest, and that's what they did. Once they were inside the bath-house, Styr sealed it off, heaping stones on top of the trap-door leading up from the bath, and in front of it he spread a wet ox-hide. Then he had plenty of water poured in through the skylight above the hearth, and this made the room so unbearably hot that the berserks couldn't stand it and started attacking the door. Halli managed to smash through and scramble outside, but he slipped on the ox-hide, and Styr gave him his death-wound. When Leiknir came rushing out through the door, Styr drove a spear through him, and he fell back dead into the bath-house. Then Styr had the bodies laid out for burial and taken over to the lava-field. There they were buried in a lava-pit so deep that nothing could be seen from the bottom except the blue sky above. This place lies close to the path.

At the berserks' burial, Styr made this verse:

> *I knew that these berserks,*
> *hardened in battle,*
> *would prove a fierce pair*
> *to me and my friends.*
> *But I'm not afraid*
> *of the fury of battle.*
> *I've put those berserks*
> *in a burial-pit.*

When Snorri heard the news, he rode off to Hraun, where he and Styr spent the whole day talking together. Afterwards they made an announcement that Asdis, Styr's Daughter, was to marry Snorri the Priest. The wedding took place in the autumn, and everyone agreed that both men had strengthened their positions by these family ties. Snorri was the shrewder of the two and a better counsellor, but Styr was more the man of action, and neither was short of kinsmen or other supporters in the district.

CHAPTER 29

A love affair

THERE WAS A MAN called Thorodd whose family belonged to Medalfell Strand. People trusted him. He was a great sea-going trader and had his own ship. Thorodd went on an Irish trading-trip to Dublin, just after Earl Sigurd Hlodvesson of Orkney had been raiding in the Hebrides and the Isle of Man.[1] The Earl forced the people of Man to pay him tribute, and once agreement had been reached, he sailed back to Orkney, leaving his agents to collect the tax, which was to be paid in refined silver. When they'd gathered the money and got everything ready, they sailed off before a south-westerly wind, but shortly after they'd set out it turned south-easterly, then easterly. Soon a strong gale blew up, and they were driven north of Ireland, where the ship was wrecked on an uninhabited island.

And that's where they were when Thorodd of Iceland found them on his way back from Dublin. The Earl's men shouted for help, so Thorodd had a boat lowered and jumped in himself. When he got to them, they pleaded with him to save them and offered him money if he'd take them back to Earl Sigurd in Orkney, but Thorodd thought he couldn't do that, as he was all set for Iceland. Still they kept pressing him, for they were convinced that their very lives and property were at stake and that the people of Ireland and the Hebrides where they'd been raiding could easily make slaves of them. So in the end Thorodd agreed to sell them his tow-boat for a large part of the tribute. The Earl's men sailed the boat to Orkney, and Thorodd carried on his voyage without a lifeboat. He made landfall in the south, then sailed west into Breida Fjord, putting in safely at Dogurdar Ness. After that, people started calling him Thorodd the Tribute-Trader.

In the autumn he went to Helgafell to stay with Snorri the Priest, shortly after the killing of Thorbjorn the Stout. Thorbjorn's widow Thurid, who was Snorri the Priest's sister, was also spending

---

1. *The History of the Earls of Orkney* (also known as *Orkneyinga Saga*) mentions Earl Sigurd's raids on the Hebrides.

the winter at Helgafell. Thorodd had been there for only a short while when he asked Snorri for his sister's hand. Snorri knew Thorodd was quite well-off and a good man too, and seeing that Thurid needed someone to take care of her, it seemed a good idea from every point of view that he should marry his sister to Thorodd. Snorri himself held the wedding-feast at Helgafell later that winter. In the spring Thorodd took over the farm at Frodriver and became a good and thrifty farmer.

No sooner had Thurid settled down at Frodriver than Bjorn Asbrandsson started calling on her, and soon the rumour got about that he was carrying on with her. Thorodd warned him off, but it didn't make any difference.

At that time Thorir Wood-Leg was farming at Arnarhvall. His sons, Orn and Val, had grown into fine men of great promise. They were critical of Thorodd for putting up with the disgrace Bjorn was causing him and offered their help, should Thorodd decide to put a stop to Bjorn's visits.

One day Bjorn came to Frodriver and settled down for a talk with Thurid. Thorodd used to stay sitting in the room until Bjorn left, but this time he was nowhere to be seen.

'Watch your step when you go back home, Bjorn,' said Thurid. 'I've a feeling Thorodd would like to make this visit your last. I think there'll be people lying in wait for you on your way home, and Thorodd will see to it the odds aren't fair when you meet.'

Then Bjorn made this verse:

> *This should be our longest day,*
> *from light golden dawn*
> *to deep blue darkness,*
> *my delight, my despair.*

Late this long day
I'll pledge a drink
to the pain-filled memory
of my passing happiness.

Bjorn took his weapons and set out for home. As he was coming up by Digramull, five men suddenly sprang up in front of him, Thorodd with two of his farmhands and the sons of Thorir Wood-Leg. They set upon Bjorn, but he defended himself with skill and courage. The Thorissons went for him fiercely and got in a number of blows, but he killed them both. Then Thorodd and his servants ran off, Thorodd only slightly wounded, and the servants not at all. Bjorn went on his way till he reached home. He went into the living-room, and his mother told a servant-maid to see to him. When she came back into the room with a light, she saw he had blood all over him, so she went to tell Asbrand, his father, that Bjorn had come home drenched in blood. Asbrand went into the room and asked Bjorn why he was bleeding so badly. 'Did you happen to run into Thorodd?' he asked. Bjorn told him he had. When Asbjorn asked him what had happened between them, Bjorn said:

'A skilful warrior,
I slaughtered Wood-Leg's sons:
harder for Thorodd
to thrust his weapon at me
than lie and make love
to his elegant lady,
or rob the Earl's traders
of all their taxes.'

After that Asbjorn dressed his wounds, and they healed completely.

Thorodd asked Snorri to support him in the action over the killing of the Thorissons, and Snorri took up his case at the Thor's Ness Assembly. The sons of Thorlak of Eyr supported Bjorn's side. The outcome was that Asbrand shook hands, gave pledges on behalf of his son Bjorn, and paid the fine for the killings, but that Bjorn was outlawed and banished from Iceland for three years. He went abroad the same summer.

That was the summer Thurid of Frodriver gave birth to a boy, who was named Kjartan. He was brought up at Frodriver and soon grew into a big promising lad.

Bjorn sailed to Norway, then south to Denmark, and from there he travelled on east to Jomsborg. At that time Palna-Toki was the leader of the Jomsvikings.[2] Bjorn joined the vikings and they thought him a great fighting-man. He was at Jomsborg when Styrbjorn the Strong conquered it, and afterwards went to Sweden when the Jomsvikings were fighting on Styrbjorn's side. He took part in the battle of Fyrisvellir when Styrbjorn was killed, but Bjorn and a number of other Jomsvikings made their escape into a forest. As long as Palna-Toki lived, Bjorn stayed with him. People considered Bjorn a great warrior and the bravest of men in every danger.

---

2. The Jomsvikings were a band of marauders who had their base near the mouth of the R. Oder on the Baltic. Their adventures are described in the semi-legendary *Jomsvikings' Saga*, but they are also mentioned in the *Heimskringla* and elsewhere in saga literature. The leaders of the Jomsvikings are said to have been killed in the Battle of Liavag in 994.

CHAPTER 30
Thorolf Twist-Foot

NOW WE COME BACK to Thorolf Twist-Foot, who was getting very old. The older he got, the more violent he became, and there was growing ill-feeling between him and his son Arnkel.

One day Thorolf rode over to Ulfarsfell to see Ulfar, a hard-working farmer who was known to be better at gathering in his hay than anyone else. Ulfar was so lucky with his livestock that not one of his beasts ever perished from disease or famine. When Thorolf met Ulfar he asked him how he should arrange the work on the farm, and whether he thought the summer would be good for drying the hay.

'The best I can do for you,' said Ulfar, 'is to tell you how I'll go about things myself. I'm having the scythes taken out today and then we'll mow all the hay we can till the end of the week, for I think it's going to rain heavily. After that there should be a good drying spell for a fortnight.'

He could foretell the weather more accurately than anyone else, so it turned out just as he'd predicted.

Thorolf went back home. He had several farmhands and told them to start with the hay-making at once, and the weather turned out just as Ulfar had said. Thorolf and Ulfar had joint ownership of a meadow up on the ridge. They both had a lot of hay there, which they were drying and gathering into large stacks. Early one morning when Thorolf got up, it was so cloudy he thought there wouldn't be any drying that day, so he told his slaves to get ready and work at stacking the hay. He said they were to keep at it all day and do their best. 'The weather seems very unsettled,' he said.

The slaves got dressed and set to work with Thorolf stacking the hay, urging them on to work harder and finish the job.

Ulfar got up early that morning to take a look round, and when he came back inside, the farmhands asked what the weather was like. He told them to go back to sleep. 'The weather's fine,' he said, 'it'll clear up. Today I want you to mow the home meadow, and then we'll gather in the hay on the ridge tomorrow.' The weather turned out just as he'd said it would, and in the evening he sent one of his farmhands up to the ridge to take a look at his haystacks there. During the day Thorolf used three yoke of oxen to cart the hay, and by the early afternoon it had all been brought in. Then he told his slaves to fetch Ulfar's hay as well, and they did exactly as he told them. When Ulfar's servant saw what they were doing, he ran back home with the news. Ulfar was furious, rushed up to the ridge and asked Thorolf why he was robbing him. Thorolf said he didn't care what Ulfar had to say, and kept prattling on. He became so violent that they came close to fighting. Ulfar saw the best thing he could do was to clear off, so he went to see Arnkel, told him about his loss and asked for his help, for without that there was nothing he could do. Arnkel promised to ask his father to pay damages for the hay, though he thought it very unlikely that it would make the slightest difference.

Arnkel went to see his father and said he ought to pay Ulfar for the hay he'd taken, but Thorolf replied that for a slave Ulfar was far too well-off already. Then Arnkel asked him as a personal favour to pay compensation for the hay, but Thorolf said he'd do nothing of the kind, though he might do something to make things worse for Ulfar. With that they parted.

Arnkel went back to Ulfar and told him what Thorolf had said. Ulfar thought Arnkel could have been much firmer, and said he ought to be able to make his father do what he wanted. Arnkel paid Ulfar's price for the hay, and next time he saw his father, Arnkel asked him for the money, but Thorolf gave the same bad-tempered answer as before, and they parted on angry terms. In the autumn Arnkel had seven of Thorolf's oxen taken from the mountain pasture and slaughtered for the table. Thorolf was furious and demanded payment for the oxen, but Arnkel said it was just to cover the cost of the hay he'd taken from Ulfar. This made Thorolf even more furious. He said Ulfar was the cause of all the trouble and threatened to make him pay dearly for it.

CHAPTER 31
Arson

THAT WINTER, about Christmas time, Thorolf held a great feast and gave his slaves plenty to drink. When he'd got them drunk, he talked them into going to Ulfarsfell, where they were to set fire to the house and burn Ulfar to death inside. As a reward he promised to free them. The slaves said they'd do it for the sake of their freedom, and trust him to keep his word. So six of them set out across to Ulfarsfell, where they got hold of some fire-wood, piled it up against the house, and set fire to it.

Over at Bolstad, Arnkel was drinking with his men, and just as they were going to bed they saw the fire at Ulfarsfell. They rushed over, seized the slaves, and put out the fire. The house was only slightly damaged. In the morning Arnkel had the slaves taken out to Vadilshofdi and hanged.

After that Ulfar formally made over his property to Arnkel,

who then became his legal guardian. This contract didn't please the Thorbrandssons at all, for they thought they had a claim to the property of Ulfar, since he was their freedman. This led to so much bitter feeling between them that they couldn't even hold common games any longer, though they'd always done so before. Arnkel had been the strongest player of them all, and there was only one who could compete against him, Freystein Bofi, Thorbrand's foster-son, the second strongest player there. Most people thought Freystein was really Thorbrand's own son, but that his mother was a slave-girl. He was a handsome man and very strong.

Thorolf Twist-Foot wasn't at all pleased about Arnkel killing his slaves and demanded compensation, but Arnkel wouldn't pay a penny, and this put Thorolf into an even worse temper.

One day Thorolf rode out to Helgafell to see Snorri the Priest. Snorri offered him hospitality, but Thorolf said it wasn't food he was after. 'I've come here because I want you to help me get justice,' he said. 'I think you're the leading farmer in the district, and it's up to you to put right any wrongs people have suffered around here.'

'Who's been trampling on your rights?' asked Snorri.

'My son Arnkel,' said Thorolf.

'You shouldn't complain,' said Snorri, 'you ought always to be on Arnkel's side, he's a much better man than you.'

'That's not true,' said Thorolf. 'Arnkel keeps bullying me more than ever. If you'd take action about the killing of the slaves, Snorri, and prosecute Arnkel for it, I'd be a real friend to you. I wouldn't claim more than a part of the compensation for myself.'

'I don't want to get caught in a quarrel between you and your son,' said Snorri.

'You're no friend of Arnkel's either,' said Thorolf, 'and though you think me a miser, I shan't be so stingy this time. I know you'd like to own Kraka Ness with all that woodland, the best in the whole district; and I'll formally hand it all over to you on condition you start proceedings over the killing of my slaves. I want you to press your case so hard that your standing will be greater than ever. The ones who wronged me must be put in their place. Show none of them any mercy, no matter how closely they may be related to me,'

Snorri thought it over; and, as the story goes, he wanted the woodland so badly that he claimed the land and promised to raise a court action over the killing of the slaves. Thorolf rode back home very pleased with himself, but most people had their doubts about this arrangement.

In the spring Snorri brought an action against Arnkel for the killing of the slaves and referred the case to the Thor's Ness Assembly. Both sides turned up at the Assembly in large numbers. Snorri pleaded the case, but when it came to court Arnkel asked the court to dismiss the case on the ground that the slaves were committing arson when they were caught. Snorri agreed that the slaves could have been lawfully killed at the place where they committed the crime, 'but,' he said, 'you took them over to Vadilshofdi to put them to death, and that's why compensation must be paid for them.'

In this way Snorri saved his case, and Arnkel's plea for dismissal was invalidated. Then people stepped in to reconcile them, and a settlement was made. Styr and his brother Vermund were chosen to arbitrate, and they awarded twelve ounces of silver for each slave, the entire amount to be paid up on the spot at the Assembly. When the fine had been paid, Snorri handed it all over to Thorolf, who took it and said: 'It never occurred to me when I gave you my land that you'd be so slack in following this up. I'm sure that if I'd left it to Arnkel, he'd never have treated me so badly, or paid me so little compensation for my slaves.'

'I don't see that the outcome discredits you in any way,' said Snorri, 'and I'm not staking my good name on your malice and injustice.'

'Don't worry, I'll never come to you again with my problems,' said Thorolf, 'and this trouble won't be the last to keep the neighbourhood awake.'

After that people went home from the Assembly. And if Arnkel and Snorri were unhappy about the outcome of the case, Thorolf was even more so.

CHAPTER 32

Ulfar is killed

THE STORY GOES that Orlyg of Orlygsstad fell ill, and as he grew weaker, his brother Ulfar came to sit beside his bed. Orlyg died of this illness. As soon as he was dead, Ulfar sent for Arnkel, who hurried over to Orlygsstad, and he and Ulfar took charge of the entire property there.

When the Thorbrandssons heard of Orlyg's death, they went to Orlygsstad and laid claim to the property on the grounds that everything formerly belonging to their freedman was theirs. Ulfar argued, on the other hand, that he was his brother's legal heir.

The Thorbrandssons asked Arnkel what he was going to do about it. He said that while Ulfar remained his partner, he wasn't going to let anyone rob him if he could help it. At that the Thorbrandssons went over to Helgafell to see Snorri the Priest. They asked him for help, but he said he had no intention of quarrelling with Arnkel over this, since they'd been so slack as to let Arnkel and Ulfar be the first to lay hands on the property. The Thorbrandssons said that Snorri would be finished when it came to bigger issues, if he didn't bother about this one.

In the autumn Arnkel held a great feast. He used to invite his friend Ulfar to these occasions and always gave him parting gifts when he left. On the last day of the feast at Bolstad, Thorolf Twist-Foot set off on a journey to see his friend Spa-Gils, who was living at Spagilsstad in Thorsardale, and asked him to ride with him up to Ulfarsfellshals. Thorolf had a slave with him. Once they were up on the ridge, Thorolf said, 'That must be Ulfar there, on his way back from the feast, and he'll be loaded with fine gifts. Spa-Gils, I want you to go and ambush him at the dyke at Ulfarsfell. I want you to kill him. In return I'll give you three ounces of silver and on top of that pay compensation for the killing. And when you've killed Ulfar, you can relieve him of the fine gifts he got from Arnkel, then hurry along west from Ulfarsfell over to Kraka Ness. If anybody starts chasing after you, there's plenty of woodland for you to hide in. After that come back to me, and I'll see to it you come to no harm.'

Spa-Gils had a large family to support and badly needed the money, so he swallowed the bait. He went down to the dyke of the home meadow at Ulfarsfell, and it wasn't long before he saw Ulfar coming up from Bolstad, carrying a fine shield that Arnkel had given him and an ornamented sword. When they met, Spa-Gils asked if he could have a look at the sword, then started saying what a great fellow Ulfar was, and how he deserved to get such grand gifts from important people. Ulfar began twirling his beard and

handed over the sword and shield. Right away Spa-Gils drew the
sword and ran Ulfar through with it, then set off from Ulfarsfell as
fast as his legs would carry him in the direction of Kraka Ness.

Arnkel was standing outside when he saw this man running
along, carrying a shield he seemed to recognise. It didn't strike
him as very likely that Ulfar would ever have willingly surrendered
the shield, so he told some of his people to go after the man.

'I think I see my father's hand in this,' said Arnkel, 'and since
this man has probably killed Ulfar already, you'd better kill him
right away, whoever he is. I'd rather not set eyes on him.'

Arnkel himself took some men up to Ulfarsfell, and there they
found Ulfar's body.

Thorolf Twist-Foot had been watching Spa-Gils as he ran west
below Ulfar's Fell with the shield and guessed what must have
happened when he met Ulfar, so he turned to the slave he had
with him. 'Go east to Karsstad,' he said to him, 'and tell the
Thorbrandssons to hurry over to Ulfarsfell. Now that Ulfar's been
killed, they'd better see to it they aren't robbed of their freedman's
inheritance a second time.' After that Thorolf rode home, well
satisfied with a good day's work.

The men chasing after Spa-Gils caught up with him at a cliff
that rises above the foreshore, and there they dragged the whole
story out of him. After he'd told them everything, they killed him
and buried his body below the cliff. The sword and shield they took
and gave back to Arnkel.

Thorolf's slave came to Karsstad and gave the Thorbrandssons
his message. They set out right away for Ulfarsfell, but by the time
they arrived Arnkel was already there with a number of men. The
Thorbrandssons formally claimed Ulfar's property, but Arnkel
presented the testimony of witnesses who'd been there when Ulfar

assigned his possessions to him. Arnkel said he planned to stand firm on his right to the property, since the original agreement had never been lawfully challenged. He warned them not to make any further claims, for he'd treat the property just as if it were a part of his own inheritance.

The Thorbrandssons saw that they had no choice but to go away; so once again they went to Helgafell to tell Snorri what had happened and ask for his help. Snorri said this wasn't the first time they'd been one move behind Arnkel.

'You'll never get the property from him now that he's got his hands on everything,' said Snorri. 'It's true the farm lies just as close to you, but the stronger is bound to win. Obviously Arnkel's going to get the best of it this time, as he always does in his dealings with you. In plain words you'll just have to put up with it, the same as other people. Arnkel tramples on everybody's rights in this neighbourhood, and will do as long as he lives, however long or short his life may be.'

Thorleif Kimbi answered him. 'That's true enough, Snorri,' he said, 'you've got every excuse for not wanting to defend our rights against Arnkel. In every single quarrel with him you've been the loser, no matter what the issue.'

The Thorbrandssons went back home in an angry mood.

CHAPTER 33

Thorolf Twist-Foot dies

SNORRI THE PRIEST STARTED MAKING USE of Krakaness Wood and had plenty of trees felled there. Thorolf Twist-Foot thought he was ruining the wood and rode down to Helgafell to ask Snorri for the wood back. Thorolf claimed he'd only leased it to Snorri, not given it away. Snorri said the matter could easily be settled. All they needed was to ask the people who'd witnessed their agreement, but unless their testimony went against him, he wasn't going to hand over the woodland.

At that Thorolf went away in a rage. He rode east to Bolstad to see his son Arnkel, who gave his father a good welcome and asked why he had come.

'I've come to see you because I'm unhappy that we're not getting on so well together,' said Thorolf. 'I'd like us to put things right and be friends again, as we ought to be. It's not proper for us to be at feud like this. It strikes me that the two of us could be the leading men in the district, what with your boldness and my cunning.'

'I'd be a lot happier myself if we were on better terms,' said Arnkel.

'This is what I'd like us to do,' said Thorolf. 'Let's begin our new friendship and mark our reconciliation by claiming Krakaness Wood from Snorri the Priest. There's nothing I hate so much as the way he keeps lording it over us, and now he won't give me back the ownership of that woodland. He even claims I gave it to him as a present, and that's a downright lie.'

'It wasn't out of friendship for me you gave Snorri the wood,' said Arnkel, 'and I'm not going to let your spiteful tongue talk me into fighting him over it. I know well enough that he has no legal right to it, but I won't have you with your ugly nature gloating over a quarrel between Snorri and me.'

'I can think of another reason,' said Thorolf. 'It's not that you grudge me the pleasure of seeing you fight it out, it's your cowardly spirit that's to blame.'

'Think whatever you like,' said Arnkel, 'I'm not starting a quarrel with Snorri over this woodland.'

With that they parted. Thorolf went back home in a fury, because he saw how difficult it was going to be for him to get what he wanted. It was evening when he got back home, and he sat down on the high-seat without uttering a word to anybody. He didn't eat all evening and stayed in his seat when the rest of the household went to bed. In the morning, when they got up, Thorolf was still sitting there, dead.

Thorolf's widow sent someone to Arnkel to tell him his father had died, so Arnkel rode over to Hvamm with some of his servants. When they got there, his father was still sitting on the high-seat, and Arnkel made sure he was really dead. Everyone in the house was numbed with fear, his death was so ugly. Arnkel went into the living-room and across the hall to get behind Thorolf. He warned everyone to be careful not to go in front of the corpse until the eyes had been closed. Then he took Thorolf by the shoulders and had to use all his strength before he could force him down. After that he wrapped some clothes around Thorolf's head and got him ready for burial according to the custom of the time. He had a hole broken through the wall behind Thorolf and the corpse was dragged outside. After he'd had a yoke of oxen hitched to a sled Arnkel laid Thorolf on it, and they started driving it up through Thorsardale, though it was hard work hauling Thorolf to his burial-place. When they got him there, they built a solid cairn over him.

After that Arnkel went back to Hvamm and took over everything his father had owned. He stayed for three days, and nothing unusual happened while he was there. Then he went back home.

CHAPTER 34

Thorolf's ghost

AFTER THOROLF DIED a good many people began finding it more and more unpleasant to stay out of doors once the sun had begun to go down. As the summer wore on, it became clear that Thorolf wasn't lying quiet, because after sunset no-one out of doors was left in peace. There was another thing, too: the oxen which had been used to haul Thorolf's body were ridden to death by demons, and every single beast that came near his grave went raving mad and howled itself to death. The shepherd at Hvamm often came racing home with Thorolf after him. One day that autumn neither sheep nor shepherd came back to the farm, and next morning, when a search was made for him, the shepherd was found dead not far from Thorolf's grave, his corpse coal-black, and every bone in his body broken. They buried him close to Thorolf. All the sheep in the valley were found dead, and the rest that had strayed into the mountains were never seen again. Any bird that happened to land on Thorolf's cairn dropped dead on the spot. All this got to be so serious that no one would risk using the valley for grazing any longer.

At night the people at Hvamm used to hear loud noises from outside, and it often sounded to them as if there was somebody sitting astride the roof. That winter, Thorolf often appeared on the farm, haunting his widow most of all. A lot of people suffered badly from it, but she was almost driven out of her wits. Eventually the strain of it killed her, and her body was taken up to Thorsardale to be buried beside Thorolf's cairn. After that the people of Hvamm abandoned the farm.

Thorolf now started haunting all over the valley, and most of the farms were deserted because of it. His ghost was so malignant that it even killed some people, and others only escaped with their lives by running away. All the people who died were later seen in his company.

Everyone complained about being terrorised like this and thought it was up to Arnkel to put a stop to it. People who thought it safer to be with Arnkel than anywhere else were invited to stay at his farm, for Thorolf and his retinue never did any harm when Arnkel was around. As the winter wore on, people grew so terrified of Thorolf's ghost that they were too scared to travel anywhere, no matter how urgent their business.

The winter passed. Spring brought fine weather; and when all the frost in the ground had thawed, Arnkel sent a messenger over to Karsstad asking the Thorbrandssons to come and help him carry Thorolf away from Thorsardale and find him another resting-place. It was the law in those days, just as it is now, that everybody must help to bury the dead if he was asked for his assistance. All the same, when word reached the Thorbrandssons, they said they had no reason to help Arnkel and his men out of their troubles. But their father Thorbrand said, 'You ought to do whatever the law requires. What you've been asked to do is something you mustn't refuse.'

So Thorodd said to the messenger, 'Go and tell Arnkel that I'll stand in for my brothers. I'll go up to Ulfar's Fell and meet him there.'

The messenger went back and told Arnkel. He got ready right away and set out with eleven men, a few oxen, and some tools for digging. First they went up to Ulfar's Fell, where Thorodd Thorbrandsson joined them with two more men. Then they all travelled together across the ridge into Thorsardale and up to Thorolf's cairn. When they broke into the cairn they saw his body was uncorrupted and very ugly-looking. They dragged him out of the grave, laid him on the sled, hitched up a powerful pair of oxen, and hauled him up to Ulfarsfellshals. By that time the oxen were so exhausted they had to get another yoke of them to haul the corpse west along the ridge. Arnkel wanted to take Thorolf all the way to Vadilshofdi and bury him there, but when they came to the end of the ridge, the oxen turned frantic and broke loose. They started racing down the ridge, then north by the hillside, past the farmstead at Ulfarsfell, and so down to the sea, where they both foundered. By now Thorolf had grown so heavy that the men could hardly shift him, but they managed to drag him up to a small knoll nearby, and there they buried him. This place has been known as Bægisfotshofdi[1] ever since. After that Arnkel had a wall built, right across the knoll, just behind the grave, and so high that only a bird in flight could get over it. At this spot Thorolf rested quietly enough as long as Arnkel lived. You can still see traces of the wall there.

CHAPTER 35

New troubles

SNORRI THE PRIEST HAD IGNORED Thorolf's protests and continued to use Krakaness Wood, but Arnkel soon made it clear that, in his opinion, Snorri had no legal right to it, and that

---

1. Lit. "Twist-Foot's knoll".

by handing it over to him Thorolf had cheated his rightful heirs.

One summer Snorri sent his slaves to work in the wood. They felled a great deal of timber, stacked it up, and then went back home. When the timber had begun to dry, Arnkel said he was going to have it collected. In fact, he didn't, but instead asked his shepherd to find out and let him know when Snorri sent for it. When the timber was completely dry, Snorri sent three of his slaves for it and told his friend Hauk to go along with them for support. So they all set off, loaded the timber on twelve packhorses, and started back home.

Arnkel's shepherd had been keeping an eye on their movements and told his master about them. Arnkel took up his weapons and set out after the slaves. He caught up with them at a place between the Svelg River and Holar. As Arnkel came up behind, Hauk jumped from his horse and made a lunge with his spear at him. The spear-thrust landed on the shield; so he wasn't hurt, but jumped off his horse and drove his own spear right into Hauk's belly. The place where Hauk died has been known as the Hauka River ever since. When the slaves saw that Hauk had been killed, they ran off towards home, and Arnkel chased them as far as the other side of Oxnabrekkur. There he turned back and drove the pack-horses up to his own farmstead. He unloaded the timber, fixed the ropes on the pack-saddles, then set the horses free, and had them driven west along the hillside, to make their own way back to Helgafell. The news spread, but nothing else happened, and things stayed quiet for the rest of the year.

In the spring Snorri the Priest brought a court action over Hauk's killing at the Thor's Ness Assembly, but Arnkel brought a counter-plea that since Hauk had been guilty of unlawful assault on him, no compensation should be paid. Both sides turned up at the Assembly in large numbers, and fought a hard case. It was decided that since Hauk had been guilty of an unlawful assault, no compensation should be paid for him. So Snorri lost his case. After that people rode back home from the Assembly: but for the rest of the summer things stayed tense.

CHAPTER 36

Attempts on Arnkel's life

A MAN CALLED THORLEIF from the East Fjords had been found guilty of seduction and outlawed. He came to Helgafell in the autumn and asked Snorri the Priest to take him in. Snorri turned him away, but had a long talk with him before he left.

Thorleif went off to Bolstad, arrived there in the evening, and stayed for two nights. Next morning Arnkel was up early repairing the main door, when Thorleif got up and asked to be taken into the household. Arnkel wasn't very keen on it and asked if he'd seen Snorri the Priest.

'I've seen him,' said Thorleif, 'and he wouldn't have me on any account. But I don't like the idea of staying with someone who's always likely to be on the losing side in everything he does.'

'I shouldn't have thought it much of a bargain for Snorri to give you food in return for your support,' said Arnkel.

'I'd much rather stay here with you,' said Thorleif.

'It's not my custom to take in strangers,' said Arnkel.

They talked the matter over for a while. Thorleif went on and on about it, while Arnkel tried to get rid of him. By this time, Arnkel had started drilling a hole through the door-plank and had laid his adze to one side. Thorleif grabbed it quickly, lifted it in the air and tried to drive it into Arnkel's head, but Arnkel heard the whizz of the blow and dived away from it. Then he heaved Thorleif up on his chest and soon showed him which of them was the stronger. Arnkel was a powerful man. He threw Thorleif down so hard that he was knocked almost senseless and dropped the adze. Arnkel picked it up and, smashing it into Thorleif's head, struck him dead.

The rumour soon got about that Snorri the Priest had sent this man to get rid of Arnkel, but Snorri let people say whatever they liked. The rest of the year passed without any further incidents.

CHAPTER 37
Arnkel is murdered

NEXT AUTUMN, at Winter Eves,[1] Snorri the Priest gave a great feast and invited all his friends. The guests were served with ale, and there was plenty of drinking and merry-making. During the feast, people started comparing the farmers in the district and arguing which of them was the best man or the greatest chieftain, and, as so often happens when people's talents are being compared, there was plenty to disagree about. Most of

---

1. *Vetrnœtr*. The Icelandic calendar divides the year into two seasons, summer and winter. The summer always begins on a Thursday in late April, and ends on a Wednesday late in October; the winter begins on the following Saturday, and the "Winter Eves" are the intervening days between the end of summer and the beginning of winter. In pagan times, sacrificial feasts used to be held about the beginning of winter.

them thought Snorri the Priest the outstanding man in the district, but others talked of Arnkel and some of Styr. While they were going on about it, Thorleif Kimbi spoke up.

'What's there to argue about?' he asked. 'We all know the truth.'

'Let's hear your opinion, then, Thorleif,' they said, 'since you're being so candid.'

'I think Arnkel's the greatest of them all,' he said.

'What makes you think that?' they asked.

'Plain facts,' he said. 'As I see it, you have to take Snorri the Priest and Styr as one person because of the way they're related. As for Arnkel, there hasn't been a single person in his household killed by Snorri without his getting compensation, and though Snorri's friend Hauk was killed by Arnkel right by Snorri's farmstead, there's been no payment for him.'

Everybody thought that although Thorleif had said no more than the truth, he'd gone too far, considering whose house they were in. So that was the end of the argument.

As the guests were setting off from the feast, Snorri chose gifts for his friends. He went to see the Thorbrandssons off and walked them down to their ship at Raudavik Head. As they parted, Snorri had a word with Thorleif Kimbi. 'Here's an axe I'd like to give you,' he said. 'It happens to be the one with the longest handle, though it won't be long enough to reach Arnkel's head, if you should ride home to Alftafjord and then try to strike him when he's stacking his hay at Orlygsstad.'

Thorleif took the axe.

'I tell you,' he said, 'I shan't be slow to swing the axe at Arnkel's head, once you've made up your mind to take revenge for your friend Hauk.'

'I think you Thorbrandssons owe it to me,' said Snorri, 'to keep your eyes open and warn me of the right moment to go for Arnkel. If I don't join you then, when there's a chance to do something and you've given me due warning, that will be the time to start blaming me.'

With that they parted, having pledged themselves to kill Arnkel. It was up to the Thorbrandssons to keep watch on his movements.

Winter set in early with heavy frost, and all the fjords were soon frozen over. Freystein Bofi was herding sheep at Alftafjord and was supposed to watch out for a chance to get at Arnkel.

Arnkel was a very hardworking man himself and used to make his slaves work, too, every day from sunrise to sunset. By now he was running the farms at Ulfarsfell and Orlygsstad, no-one else being willing to farm there for fear of the Thorbrandssons. During the winter Arnkel used to go to Orlygsstad by moonlight for supplies of hay, but kept the slaves busy with other work during the day. That the Thorbrandssons could watch him go to haul in the hay didn't bother him in the least.

One night just before Christmas Arnkel got up, roused three of his slaves, one of them called Ofeig, and went with them up to Orlygsstad along with four oxen and two sleds. The Thorbrandssons got to know about it, and that same night Freystein Bofi set off over the ice west to Helgafell. When he got there, everyone had been in bed for some time. He roused Snorri the Priest, who asked what he wanted.

'The old eagle's flown over to Orlygsstad for his prey.' said Freystein.

Snorri got up and told his men to dress, and when they were ready they took up their weapons. Nine of them set off over the ice to Alfta Fjord. The Thorbrandssons joined them at the head of the fjord, and there were six in that group. They all went up to Orlygsstad and got there just after one of the slaves had left with a hay-load. Arnkel and the two other slaves were busy getting the next one ready, when they saw the armed men walking up from the foreshore. Ofeig said this could only mean trouble. 'Our one chance is to get back to the farm,' he said.

'I'll tell you what,' said Arnkel. 'We'll each have to do whatever we think best. You two run back home and rouse my men, and they'll be here in no time. The haystack's a good place to defend myself, so I'll take my stand here if these men are on the warpath. I'd rather fight than run. They'll find me a hard man to put down, and, if you do just as I tell you, my men won't be long coming.'

As soon as Arnkel had finished speaking, the slaves set off running. Ofeig was the faster, and he was scared almost out of his wits. As he went racing up the mountain he fell over a waterfall, and that was the end of him. The place is still called Ofeig's Falls. The other slave ran all the way home. When he came to the barn, one of his fellow-slaves who was carrying in the hay shouted and asked him to give a hand. The slave started helping right away, and he'd obviously no objection to the work.

Now we go back to Arnkel. He'd recognised Snorri the Priest and others in the group, so he tore the runner off the sled and pulled it up on to the haystack. The outer turf wall was high, sloping up very steeply inwards, and the hay nearest to it had been cleared away. The place looked as safe as a fortress.

Snorri and his men came up to the haystack, and it is not said that many words passed between them. They set on Arnkel at once, attacking him mostly with spears, but he warded them off with the sled-runner and kept breaking their spearshafts, so he wasn't hurt at all. When they'd run out of missiles, Thorleif Kimbi tried scaling the wall with his sword drawn, but Arnkel struck out with the runner, and he had to jump down to dodge the blow. As the runner hit the wall, it broke the frozen turf sods and cracked at the mortise, so that one part of it fell down outside the wall. Arnkel had left his sword and shield lying in the hay, and now he took them up to defend himself. He'd soon been wounded several times, but as the attackers closed in, forcing their way inside the wall, he scrambled higher up the stack. There he made his last stand, but in the end they killed him and covered his body with hay. Then Snorri took the men back to Helgafell.

Thormod Trefilsson made this verse about the killing of Arnkel:

> *When the battle-hard*
> *hero was yet young*
> *he gained the victory,*
> *gorging the ravens.*
> *But Snorri's sword-blade*
> *split open the breast*
> *of the brave Arnkel;*
> *that was his death-blow.*

Coming back now to Arnkel's slaves, they finished carrying in the hay and went into the house. As they were getting out of their hide working-clothes, Arnkel's men woke up and asked where he was. The slave acted just as if he'd been roused from a dream.

'The fact is,' he said, 'Arnkel must be fighting with Snorri the Priest by now, over at Orlygsstad.'

The men jumped to their feet, got into their clothes and rushed over to Orlygsstad, but found Arnkel, their master, dead. Arnkel was mourned by everyone, for of all men in pagan times he was the most gifted. He was outstandingly shrewd in judgment, good-tempered, kind-hearted, brave, honest, and moderate. He came out on top in every law-suit, no matter who he was dealing with, and that's why people were so envious of him, as the manner of his death proves.

Arnkel's men took his body and laid it out for burial. A mound was raised for him at Vadilshofdi as big as a large haystack and close by the sea.

CHAPTER 38

Settlement

ON ARNKEL'S DEATH, the legal heirs to his estate were all women, and it was their duty to take action over the killing. Consequently the case was not followed up as vigorously as people might have expected after the killing of so great a man. The case was settled at the Assembly, and Thorleif Kimbi was the only one to be sentenced to outlawry. He was charged with giving Arnkel his death-wound and banished from Iceland for three years. Because the action over the killing of this outstanding man had gone so badly, the leading men of Iceland made it law that neither a woman, nor a man under the age of sixteen, should ever again be allowed to raise a manslaughter action, and this has been the law ever since.

CHAPTER 39

A new dispute

THAT SAME SUMMER Thorleif Kimbi arranged for his passage
with some traders who were getting their ship ready in Straum
Fjord, and their leaders invited him to take meals with them. In
those days it wasn't usual for traders to have cooks aboard, but
all those who shared a table used to cast lots from day to day to
decide which of them should do the cooking. There was a common
supply of water for the whole crew from a cask with a lid on it,
which stood near the mast. Extra water was kept in barrels and
emptied into the cask as the water there was used up.

As they were just about to set sail, a stranger came down to
Budarhamar. He was a tall man, carrying a bundle on his back,
and there was something out of the ordinary about him. He asked
for the skipper and was shown to his tent. The stranger laid his
luggage down by the tent door and went inside. He asked the
skipper if he would take him abroad. When they asked him his
name, he said he was Arnbjorn Asbrandsson of Kamb and wanted
to go abroad to look for his brother Bjorn, who had left the country
some years before, and about whom nothing had been heard since
he went to Denmark. The traders said they'd already covered up
the cargo and didn't want to re-open it. Arnbjorn pointed out that
he had so little baggage that it could easily be placed on top of the
cargo. It seemed to them that he had urgent reasons for going
overseas, so they took him aboard. As he was by himself and didn't
share meals with anybody, he was given a berth in the bows. His
baggage consisted of three hundred ells of home-spun cloth,

twelve sheep-skins, and food for the voyage. Arnbjorn proved very handy and helpful, and the traders came to like him a lot.

They had a good passage, and after they made landfall in Hordaland, they sailed up to a rocky island and went ashore to cook a meal. It was Thorleif's turn to do the cooking, and he was supposed to make porridge. Arnbjorn was already ashore, cooking porridge for himself in the pot that Thorleif was to use after him. Thorleif went ashore and told Arnbjorn to give him the pot, but the porridge wasn't quite ready, and Arnbjorn stirred away, refusing to budge. The Norwegians on board started shouting at Thorleif, telling him to get on with the cooking. They said he was just like all the other Icelanders, far too slow at everything. Thorleif got into a temper, grabbed the pot and flung it down, spilling Arnbjorn's porridge. But, as Thorleif started walking away, Arnbjorn hit him on the neck with the ladle, which he still had in his hand. It wasn't a hard blow, but the ladle was hot with the porridge and burnt Thorleif's neck.

'Since we're the only Icelanders here,' said Thorleif, 'it wouldn't be right to give the Norwegians a chance to make fun of us, then drag us apart like a pair of fighting dogs. But I'll remember this next time we meet back in Iceland.' Arnbjorn didn't answer.

They lay there at anchor for some days till they got a favourable wind to take them up to the mainland, and there they unloaded the cargo. Thorleif found lodgings, but Arnbjorn fixed himself a passage on a cargo-boat bound for Oslo Fjord. From there he sailed to Denmark and started looking for his brother Bjorn.

CHAPTER 40

Bjorn comes back to Iceland

THORLEIF KIMBI SPENT TWO YEARS in Norway, then went
back to Iceland with the same traders. They made landfall at
Breida Fjord and sailed up to Dogurdar Ness. Thorleif came home
to Alftafjord in the autumn, and was as pleased with himself as
ever.

That same summer Bjorn and his brother Arnbjorn also came
back to Iceland, and landed at Hraunhaven Mouth. By this time
Bjorn had got the nickname of Breidavik-Champion. Arnbjorn
came back with a good deal of money, and shortly afterwards
bought some land at Bakki in Hraun Haven. He started farming
there the following spring after having spent the winter with his
brother-in-law, Thord Blig. Arnbjorn wasn't much of a one for
display and didn't have a lot to say for himself, but he was a very
brave man all the same. His brother Bjorn, on the other hand, was
a great one for show, and after he came back to Iceland he used to
dress well, having modelled himself on some of the great men
overseas. He was also a much more handsome man than Arnbjorn,
but he wasn't any less brave, and he'd picked up a lot of experience
in fighting while he was abroad.

That summer, just after they'd come back, there was a crowded
meeting at Haugabrekkur east of the mouth of the Frod River on
the north side of the moor. The traders came to it on horseback, all
dressed in brightly-coloured clothes, and by the time they arrived
a lot of people had already gathered. Among them was Thurid,
the housewife at Frodriver, and Bjorn went over to talk to her.
No-one thought anything of it. It seemed only natural that they

should have plenty to chat about when they hadn't seen each other for such a long time.

Later in the day a fight broke out at the meeting, and one of the men from the north side got a fatal wound. People carried him into a willow copse on the flats by the river. The wound was bleeding freely, and a pool of blood formed beside the thicket. Young Kjartan, Thurid's son, had a small axe in his hand. He ran up to the willows and dipped the axe in the blood.

After the meeting, when the people from the south were riding back home, Thord Blig asked Bjorn how he had got on with Thurid, and Bjorn said he was quite pleased with the talk they'd had. Thord asked if he had noticed young Kjartan, the son of Thurid, Thorodd (and someone else!).

'I saw him,' said Bjorn.

'What do you think of him, then?' asked Thord, and Bjorn replied with this verse:

> *'I saw the boy,*
> *eyes blazing,*
> *pace like a wolf to the pool*
> *of blood by the willows.*
> *Though he's my living image,*
> *little he knows*
> *that one who once steered a longship*
> *is his sea-faring father.'*

'Thorodd must be wondering whether he's the boy's father or you are.' said Thord, and Bjorn made another verse:

'The slim, high-born lady
who bears Thorodd's stoutness,
loved me once, sweetly,
with her soft body.
Brooding I yearn
that her body might breed
other fine boys like one
born in my image.'

'Better not have anything more to do with Thurid,' said Thord: 'try to forget her.'

'That makes sense,' said Bjorn, 'but my heart tells me otherwise, though I know I'll be up against someone I'm no match for, and that's her brother, Snorri the Priest.'

'Take care of yourself,' said Thord, and that was the end of their talk.

Bjorn went to live at Kamb and took charge of the farm, as his father was dead by this time. In the winter he set off north across the moor to see Thurid. Thorodd took it very badly, but didn't know what he could do about it. He kept thinking of the rough time the two of them had given him before when he complained about how they were carrying on. Now he realised that Bjorn was a more formidable rival than ever. That winter Thorodd gave Thorgrima Witch-Face some money to work a spell and cause a blizzard when Bjorn was crossing the moor.

One day Bjorn went over to Frodriver, and in the evening when he started back, the sky was overcast, and it rained a little. He was late leaving, and by the time he got up to the moor the weather had grown colder, and snow was drifting. It soon grew too dark for him to see the path, and then a blizzard blew up, so violent that he could hardly stay on his feet. He'd been soaked to the skin, and now his clothes began to freeze, he had lost his bearings and had no idea where he was going. During the night he came upon a cave and crawled inside to shelter there till morning, but it was cold comfort. Then he made this verse:

> *The woman sleeping*
> *warm in her wide bed*
> *would shiver with pity*
> *if she saw my plight;*
> *alone her friend*
> *the seafarer must lie here,*
> *cold without comfort*
> *in his rocky cave.*

He added another:

> *Since she gave me*
> *her love, I've sailed*
> *my laden ship*
> *through frozen seas;*
> *many a burden*
> *I've borne with courage;*
> *now I've bartered*
> *her bed for this cavern.*

Bjorn spent three days in the cave before the weather cleared up. On the fourth day he made his way down from the moor and back home to Kamb, absolutely worn out. People asked him where he'd been during the blizzard, and he made this verse:

'You've heard of my bravery
under Styrbjorn's banner
when the steel-clad Eirik
stalked, wading through blood?
But now I've been wandering
about in the wilderness,
losing my way back
in that weird blizzard.'

Bjorn stayed at home for the rest of the winter. In the spring his brother Arnbjorn started farming at Bakki in Hraun Haven, but Bjorn went on living at Kamb and ran a splendid farm.

CHAPTER 41

A marriage offer

THAT SPRING at the Thor's Ness Assembly, Thorleif Kimbi made an offer of marriage and asked for the hand of Helga, Thorlak's daughter, sister of Steinthor of Eyr. Her brother Thormod was strongly in favour of this, as he was married to Thorleif Kimbi's sister Thorgerd: but when Steinthor was told, he didn't seem very enthusiastic and asked his brothers what they thought about it. First they went to Thord Blig, and when the matter was put to him, this is what he said:

'I'm not waiting to hear what other people want, and I shan't mince my words. I'll tell you this to your face, Thorleif, I'll never see my sister married to you until the scars are healed that you got on your neck from that porridge in Norway three years ago.'

'I'm not sure what can be done about that,' said Thorleif, 'and I doubt if I'll be able to get my revenge. But I'll say this: before the next three years are out, I'd very much like to see you get a knock yourself.'

'You don't scare me a bit with your threats,' said Thord.

Next morning there was a turf-game[1] going on near the Thorbrandsson's tent. The Thorlakssons happened to be passing by, when a great lump of sandy turf came flying through the air and caught Thord Blig on the neck, hitting him so hard that he went head over heels. When he got back on his feet again, he could see the Thorbrandssons laughing at him. The Thorlakssons turned round with their swords drawn, and the two sides faced up to each other and started fighting. Several men were wounded, but no-one was killed. Steinthor wasn't involved, as he was off somewhere else talking with Snorri the Priest. The fighters were separated, and people tried to arrange a settlement. In the end it was agreed that Snorri and Steinthor should arbitrate, and their verdict was that the wounds on either side and the unlawful assault should cancel each other out, with compensation to be paid where things needed to be evened up. So when they rode back home, they'd more or less come to terms.

---

1. This game is not mentioned anywhere else; and how it was played is not known.

CHAPTER 42

An attempt
on Arnbjorn's life

THAT SUMMER A SHIP PUT IN at Hraunhaven Mouth, and another at Dogurdar Ness. Snorri the Priest had some business with the ship at Hraun Haven, so he rode off with fourteen companions. As they were coming south over the moor on their way into Dufgusdale, six fully-armed men came after them, riding hard. It was the Thorbrandssons. When Snorri asked where they were heading, they said they were on their way to the ship at Hraunhaven Mouth. Snorri offered to look after their business there. He asked them to go back home and take care not to provoke anyone, as very little was needed to spark off trouble between people on uneasy terms should they happen to meet.

'No-one's going to say we're too frightened of the men of Breidavik to travel through the district,' said Thorleif Kimbi. 'Of course, you can ride back home yourself, if you're too timid to go about your own business.'

Snorri didn't answer, and together they rode on across the ridges west to Hofgardar, and from there by the sea-route over the sands. As they were coming towards the estuary, the Thorbrandssons turned off up towards Bakki and dismounted at the farmstead. They tried to force their way into the house, but couldn't break open the door, so they climbed on to the roof and started tearing it up. Inside the house, Arnbjorn had his weapons ready to defend himself. He kept thrusting his spear through the roof, and his attackers suffered a number of wounds. It was early morning, and the day was fine and sunny.

That same morning the men of Breidavik had got up early and set off towards the ship. As they were passing Oxl, they noticed someone in bright clothes on top of the farmhouse roof at Bakki. They knew it wasn't Arnbjorn's style of dress, so Bjorn and his men rode up to the farmstead.

As soon as Snorri the Priest realised the Thorbrandssons weren't with him any longer, he rode back after them; and when he and his men came to Bakki, the Thorbrandssons were still busy trying to break through the roof. Snorri told the brothers to clear off and not cause any trouble as long as they were with him. Since they hadn't managed to get into the house, they did as they were told, gave up the attack, and rode with him down to the ship.

The men of Breidavik got to the ship later in the day. The two sides kept out of each other's way, and though there was a lot of strain and tension between them, they didn't come to blows. The men of Breidavik outnumbered their opponents at the market. In the evening Snorri the Priest rode south to Hofgardar, where Bjorn and his son Gest were living at the time – Gest was the father of Hofgardar-Ref. Bjorn the Breidavik-Champion and his men told Arnbjorn they were ready to ride after Snorri, but Arnbjorn didn't want it and said it would be best if both sides were to rest content with the points they'd scored already. Snorri and his party rode back home the following day, the Thorbrandssons even more unhappy about things than before. So the autumn passed.

CHAPTER 43

The price of a slave

THORBRAND OF ALFTAFJORD had a slave called Egil the Strong, a man of exceptional size and strength. He didn't like being a slave, so he kept begging Thorbrand and his sons to give him his freedom, and said he'd do anything within his power to repay them. One evening Egil went to herd his sheep between Alfta Fjord and Borgardale. It was getting very late, when he saw an eagle come flying east across the fjord. Egil had a big foxhound with him. The eagle came swooping down, picked up the dog in its talons, and flew with it west across the fjord to Thorolf's grave. Then the eagle flew on and vanished behind the mountain. Thorbrand said it was an omen that something was about to happen.

At Winter Eves it was the custom of the Breidavik people to hold ball-games just below Oxl Mountain, south of Knorr, and the place is still known as the Leikskalar Fields.[1] People from all over the district used to come to these games in crowds, and large shelters were built for them there, as some of them would stay for a fortnight or even longer. At that time there were a good many people living in the district, among them some very fine men. Most of the younger men took part in the games, but not Thord Blig. It wasn't his strength, it was his aggressiveness, that made them keep him out of the games, so he used to sit on a stool and watch

---

1. *Leik-skálar*, lit. "playing-sheds". These ball games were played in winter, on ice. A wooden ball was used, and the object of the game seems to have been to get the ball across the opponents' line: but the rules are not known in detail.

the play. Bjorn and his brother Arnbjorn were so strong that people thought they shouldn't play unless they competed against each other.

That same autumn the Thorbrandssons told their slave Egil to go to the ball-games and find some way to kill one of the Breidavik men, either Bjorn, Arnbjorn, or Thord. In return they promised him his freedom. Some people think that Snorri the Priest was behind the plot, and that it was his idea that the slave should hide in the shed and attack his victim there. Snorri is said to have told the slave to wait in the mountain pass above Leikskalar and not go down from there till the fires had been lit, as there is usually a sea-breeze in the evening which would carry the smoke up to the mountain pass. People say he warned Egil to wait there and not go down till the mountain pass had filled with smoke.

Egil set out on his mission. First he travelled west to the fjords, where he kept asking about the Alftafjord sheep and pretended to be searching for them, though Freystein Bofi was herding them all the time at Alftafjord.

In the evening, after Egil had gone, Freystein went across the river to keep an eye on the sheep, and when he came west of the river to the scree called Geirvor, right out in the open he saw a severed human head. The head was chanting this verse:

> *'Geirvor's lips are red*
> *with human blood;*
> *soon she'll be kissing*
> *human heads.'*[2]

---

2. *Geirvör* is a well-known woman's name: the second element, *vör*, can also mean a "lip".

He told Thorbrand about this, and he thought it very ominous.

Meanwhile Egil kept on the move, west through the fjords, up the mountain east of Buland Head, then south straight across the mountain into the pass above Leikskalar, and there he hid for the rest of the day, watching the games being played.

Thord Blig wasn't taking part, but was sitting at the games. 'I can't tell what it is I keep seeing up there in the pass,' he said. 'Either it's a bird or someone in hiding. It keeps bobbing up and down. It must be alive. I think it would be a good idea to take a closer look.' But nobody did anything about it.

That day it was the turn of Bjorn the Breidavik-Champion and Thord Blig to do the chores at the shed. Bjorn's job was to light the fire and Thord's to fetch the water. When he had the fire going, the smoke started drifting up to the mountain pass, just as Snorri had said it would, and Egil set off down to the shed under cover of the smoke. The games were still on, though it was getting very late. The fire was blazing away, and when the shed was full of smoke, Egil made his way down to it. He was wearing shoes with tasselled thongs, as people did in those days, and one of the thongs came undone, so the tassel was trailing behind him as he walked into the big shed. He tried to tread as softly as he could, for he'd already caught a glimpse of Thord and Bjorn sitting by the fire, and thought he had lifelong freedom within his grasp. But as he crossed the doorsill, he stepped on the loose tassel. He tried to move the other foot, but the tassel was caught, so that he tripped and crashed on to the floor with a great thump, sounding just like the carcase of a skinned bull. Thord leapt to his feet and asked who the devil was there. Bjorn was up, too, and pounced on Egil. Before he could get to his feet, Bjorn had grabbed hold of him and was asking him his name.

'It's Egil, friend,' said the slave.

'Egil who?' asked Bjorn.

'Egil of Alftafjord,' he said.

Thord picked up a sword, and would have killed him, if Bjorn hadn't held him back and told him not to do anything yet. 'First we must get the whole story out of him,' he said.

They shackled Egil by the feet; and when people came back to the shed in the evening, Egil told all of them what he'd been sent to do. They kept him there overnight, and in the morning took him up to the pass and killed him. Nowadays the place is called Egilsskard.[3]

It was the law in those days that anyone who killed someone else's slave was to bring the owner twelve ounces of silver to his home in compensation. He should set out not later than sunrise on the third day after the killing. Once this payment had been properly made, no legal action could be taken.

After they'd put Egil to death, the Breidavik brothers decided to hand over compensation, as the law demanded. They set out from Leikskalar with thirty hand-picked men and rode north over the moor to see Steinthor of Eyr, where they stayed overnight. He came along with them, and by the time they set off from Eyr they were sixty strong. They rode east by the fjords and spent the next night at Bakki with Steinthor's brother Thormod. They asked their kinsmen Styr and Vermund to join them, so by now there were eighty of them altogether. Steinthor sent someone over to Helgafell to see what Snorri would do when he found out about the force they'd gathered. When the spy came to Helgafell, Snorri was sitting in the high-seat, and there was nothing out of the ordinary

---

3. Lit. "Egil's pass".

to show what Snorri was planning to do. He returned to Bakki and told Steinthor what he'd seen at Helgafell.

'It's just as I thought,' said Steinthor; 'Snorri would never deny us our legal rights, and if he's not going to Alftafjord, I don't see any point in taking this large force with us, for I want us to go about our business quietly and complete it legally. I think it would be a good idea if you, Thord, and the rest of the Breidavik men were to stay behind here, because the smallest thing could spark off a fight between you and the Thorbrandssons.'

'One thing's certain,' said Thord: 'I'm going. Thorleif Kimbi's not going to have an excuse to poke fun at me and say I wouldn't dare bring the slave-payment myself.'

Steinthor turned to the brothers Bjorn and Arnbjorn and said, 'I want you to stay behind with twenty men.'

'I'm not going to force you to take me along if you don't want me,' said Bjorn, 'but this is the first war-band I've ever been thrown out of. One thing I know, Snorri the Priest will outsmart you all, for though I'm no prophet, I've a feeling how your trip's going to turn out; and next time we meet, you'll be telling me you didn't have enough men with you.'

'As long as I'm in charge here, I'll follow my own counsel,' said Steinthor, 'even though I may not be as smart as Snorri the Priest.'

'You can do what you like, for all I care,' said Bjorn.

After that Steinthor set off from Bakki with nearly sixty men. They rode east across Skeid over to Drapuhlid, then on to Vatnshals, right across Svelgardale and up to Ulfarsfellshals.

CHAPTER 44

The Battle of Alfta Fjord

S NORRI THE PRIEST HAD SENT WORD asking his neighbours to move their ships to leeward of Raudavik Head; and as soon as Steinthor's spy was out of the way, he set off to join them with his men. He didn't want to go sooner, because he knew Steinthor must have sent this man to spy on him. Snorri sailed three ships up Alfta Fjord with nearly fifty men aboard, and reached Karsstad ahead of Steinthor. When they saw Steinthor's force moving towards Karsstad, the Thorbrandssons wanted to march against them and block their way into the home meadow. 'We've plenty of good fighters here,' they said. There were eighty of them all told.

'We mustn't bar them from the farmstead,' said Snorri the Priest, 'or refuse Steinthor his legal rights. I know he'll go about his business in a quiet and sensible manner, so we'll all go inside, and I don't want anybody to start bandying words with them, since that would only make matters worse.'

They went into the living-room, and all sat down on the benches except the Thorbrandssons, who kept pacing up and down the floor. Steinthor and his men came riding up to the door. People say he wore a scarlet tunic tucked into his belt at the front. He had a fine shield and helmet, and at his waist a superb ornamented sword: the hilt shone with white silver, and the grip was bound with silver wire, gold-threaded. After Steinthor and his men had dismounted, he walked up to the door, and nailed to it a purse containing twelve ounces of silver. Then he appointed witnesses to testify that he'd made lawful payment for the slave.

The door was open, and one of the women was standing there

listening to the naming of witnesses. Then she went into the room. 'That Steinthor's a fine-looking warrior,' she said. 'When he paid the compensation for the slave, he spoke really well.'

As soon as Thorleif Kimbi heard this, he rushed out of the room with his brothers, and the rest of the men followed. Thorleif was the first to get to the door. He saw Thord Blig standing outside with a shield in front of him, but Steinthor had already started off across the home meadow. Thorleif grabbed a spear standing by the door and lunged at Thord. It struck the shield, but glanced off into the shoulder, giving him a nasty wound. Now the rest of the men came running out, and a battle started in the meadow near the farmstead. Steinthor was putting up a great fight, hewing away on either side. Then Snorri the Priest came out and told them to stop. He asked Steinthor to ride out of the meadow and promised not to go after him, so Steinthor and his men cleared out of the field and the fighting ended.

As Snorri came back to the door, he saw his son Thorodd standing there with a bad shoulder wound. He was just twelve years old. Snorri asked who had given him the wound.

'Steinthor of Eyr,' said the boy.

'Steinthor seems to have done his best to pay you back for your promise not to go after him,' said Thorleif Kimbi. 'I don't think we should let him get away with this.'

'So be it,' said Snorri. 'We've not done with him yet.'

He asked Thorleif to tell the others that they were going after Steinthor and his men, who'd just got out of the home meadow when they saw the men coming after them. They crossed the river and made their way up the scree called Geirvor. It was an ideal place to make a stand because of the stones lying everywhere; and there they braced themselves for the fight. As Snorri and his men were coming up the scree. Steinthor cast a spear over them for good luck, according to ancient custom.[1] The spear sought out its victim and landed on Mar Hallvardsson, Snorri's uncle, putting him out of the fight. They told Snorri about this. 'Good,' said he: 'that shows it's not always best to walk behind.'

Then the fighting started in real earnest. Steinthor was always in front, hewing away on either side, but whenever he struck a shield, his ornamented sword would bend, and he'd have to put his foot on it to straighten it out. He did his best to get at Snorri the Priest. His kinsman Styr Thorgrimsson fought briskly at his side, and it was he who claimed the first victim when he killed one of the supporters of his own son-in-law, Snorri. When Snorri saw this he asked, 'Is this how you avenge your grandson Thorodd when he's dying of the wound Steinthor gave him? You're no better than a traitor!'

'I can soon make it up to you,' said Styr, and with that he changed sides. He joined Snorri with all his followers, and the next man he killed was one of Steinthor's.

Then Aslak of Langdale came on the scene with his son Illugi the Strong and thirty men, and tried to stop the fighting. Vermund the Slender joined with them, and they all appealed to Snorri to put an end to this slaughter. Snorri replied that it was up to the men of Eyr to come forward and make peace with him, and the mediators asked Steinthor to accept a truce on behalf of his men. Steinthor asked Snorri to shake hands on the agreement, but just

---

1. The ancient custom of casting a spear over the enemy ranks is associated elsewhere in medieval Icelandic literature with the cult of Odin, the god of war, to whom the victims were dedicated: see, *e.g.*, *Styrbjorn's Saga* and *The Sybil's Vision*.

as Snorri put forward his hand, Steinthor drew his sword and struck at it. The sword landed with a loud crack on the temple-ring and cut it almost in two, but Snorri wasn't hurt.

Thorodd Thorbrandsson shouted out, 'They'll never keep the peace, we'll have to go on fighting till all the Thorlakssons are dead.'

'There'll be plenty of trouble in this neighbourhood, if all the Thorlakssons have to die,' said Snorri the Priest; 'so if Steinthor's willing, we'd better come to terms as we've already agreed.'

Everyone pleaded with Steinthor to make peace, and in the end a truce was arranged for each man to go safely back home.

When the men of Breidavik heard that Snorri had taken a large force of men with him to Alftafjord, they set out on horseback after Steinthor, riding as hard as they could; and while the battle on the scree was being fought, they were making their way along the ridge above Ulfarsfell. Some people say that Snorri the Priest had already noticed Bjorn and his men on the ridge as he was facing that way, and that was why he was so willing to make peace with Steinthor.

After the battle Steinthor and Bjorn met at Orlygasstad, and Bjorn said it had turned out just as he'd said it would. 'What I think we should do now,' he said, 'is to turn back and hit them hard.'

'Whatever happens between us in the future,' said Steinthor, 'I'm keeping to my agreement with Snorri the Priest.'

Then they rode off each to his own home, but Thord Blig had to stay in bed at Eyr while his wounds were healing.

Five of Steinthor's men were killed in the Battle of Alfta Fjord and Snorri the Priest lost two: but a good many on both sides were wounded, for there had been bitter fighting. This is how Thormod Trefilsson described it in his *Lay of the Raven*:

The feeder of ravens
gave flesh to the eagles,
a feast fit for wolves
at Alfta Fjord!
Snorri took five
of these fighters' lives
in the flash of the war-storm:
thus were his foes punished.

Along with Aslak and Illugi, Thorbrand had been at the battle in the role of peace-maker, and it was he who asked them to seek a settlement. He thanked the other two handsomely for the help they'd given, and Snorri for his support. After the battle Snorri the Priest went back home to Helgafell. The agreement was that, until the quarrel had been settled, the Thorbrandssons should stay alternately at Helgafell or home at Alftafjord, because feeling still ran high between the two sides, and the truce was not binding once the men had got back home from the battle.

CHAPTER 45

The Battle of Vigra Fjord

AS WE HAVE SAID ALREADY, the summer before the Battle of Alfta Fjord a ship put in at Dogurdar Ness. Steinthor of Eyr had bought a fine ten-oared boat there, and as he was sailing to fetch it, he ran into a fierce westerly gale which drove him round Thor's Ness and forced him to put in at Thingskalar Ness. They hauled the boat ashore at Gruflu-Naust, and from there they travelled on foot across the hills over to Bakki and the rest of the way by sea. They didn't get round to fetching the ten-oared boat that autumn, and it lay at Gruflu-Naust, where they left it.

Early one morning just before Christmas, Steinthor got up and said he was going over to Thingskalar Ness for the boat. His brothers Bergthor and Thord Blig went with him. Thord's wounds had healed so well that he could fight again. Two Norwegians were staying with Steinthor, and they joined him on the trip, so there were eight of them altogether. First they had themselves ferried across the fjord over to Selja Head, and from there they walked on to Bakki, where their brother Thormod joined them; they were now nine strong.

Hofstad Bay was frozen over as far out as Greater Bakki, so they walked across the ice, and then over the isthmus to Vigra Fjord, which was also under ice. This fjord dries up at low tide, and then the ice settles on the mud flats, but the rocks in the fjord stick up through the ice. Slabs of broken ice were jutting up all round the rocks, and the ice was covered with a layer of fresh snow, making it very slippery indeed.

Steinthor and his men walked over to Thingskalar and hauled the boat down from the shed. They took the oars and benches from the boat, left them on the ice with their heavy weapons and clothes, and started dragging the boat north across the fjord over the isthmus to Hofstad Bay right to the edge of the ice. Then they started back to get their clothes and other things they had left behind. Just as they reached Vigra Fjord, they saw six men travelling fast across the ice from Thingskalar Ness towards Helgafell. Steinthor and his men suspected that these must be the Thorbrandssons. Steinthor's party started running across the fjord to get their clothes and weapons. As Steinthor had guessed, these were the Thorbrandssons, and when the Thorbrandssons saw people running across the fjord, they too realised who these men must be. They knew Steinthor and his men would be eager to meet with them, and they decided to make their stand. The two parties came very close to each other, but the Thorbrandssons were the first to get to the rock. As soon as Steinthor and his men came close enough, Thorleif Kimbi hurled at them a spear, which hit Bergthor Thorlaksson in the belly and put him out of the fight. Bergthor walked a few steps over the ice and lay down, but Steinthor and some of his men made an attack on the rock, while others ran back to arm themselves. The Thorbrandssons put up a sturdy defence. They were in a strong position with the slippery ice blocks on all sides of the rock, so they suffered no wounds until the others came back with the weapons. Steinthor and another five men tried a direct assault, but the Norwegians kept back so that they could shoot at the men on the rock with their bows and arrows. They soon began to wound the defenders.

Thorleif saw Steinthor drawing his sword. 'I see you're still wearing a white-hilted sword, Steinthor,' he said, 'I wonder if it's got the same blunt edge as the one you had last autumn at Alftafjord?'

'I'd like to test the sword on you before we part,' said Steinthor, 'and then we'll see how blunt it is.'

They found the rock difficult to attack. After they'd been fighting for some time, Thord Blig ran up to it and tried to lunge with a spear at Thorleif Kimbi, who was always at the front. Thorleif took the spear on his shield, but the thrust was so powerful that Thord slipped on the sloping ice block, fell backwards, and slid away down from the rock. Thorleif rushed after him with the idea of killing him before he could get back on his feet again. Wearing spiked shoes Freystein Bofi ran up to join Thorleif, and Steinthor turned sharply towards them. He flung his shield over Thord as Thorleif was about to strike, and with his other hand he took a swing at Thorleif, severing the leg just below the knee. At that same moment Freystein Bofi was aiming a thrust at Steinthor's middle, but Steinthor saw it coming and leapt in the air so that the spear went between his legs. All three things Steinthor did in a single moment, just as we've described them. Then he hewed at Freystein with his sword, and the blow landed on his neck with a loud crack.

'A nasty one, that, Freystein,' said Steinthor.

'Yes, it was,' agreed Freystein, 'but not as bad as you thought, it's not done me any harm.' He was wearing a felt hood with a piece of horn sewn on to the collar, and that's where the blow had landed.

Freystein started back to the rock, but Steinthor told him not to run if he wasn't hurt, so Freystein turned round, and they started on each other again. Steinthor kept skidding off balance because the blocks of ice were steep and slippery, while Freystein stood firm on his spikes and was able to strike hard at him again and again. But at last Steinthor got in a blow just above Freystein's hips, slicing him clean through. Then they all moved up to the rock and didn't stop till all the Thorbrandssons were down. Thord Blig wanted them to cut off the Thorbrandssons' heads, but Steinthor said he wasn't going to make war on men who were lying on their backs. So now they moved away from the rock over to where Bergthor lay. He could still talk, and they took him back with them over the ice, across the isthmus and to the boat, then rowed over to Bakki in the evening.

That day Snorri's shepherd had been at Oxnabrekkur and

could see the fighting on Vigra Fjord. He raced back home and told Snorri that a terrible battle was taking place there. Snorri and his men, nine of them altogether, took up their weapons and went over to the fjord. By the time they got there, Steinthor and his men were already away from the ice-field. When Snorri went to look at the wounded, he saw that while only Freystein Bofi was dead, all the others were so badly hurt that they seemed unlikely to live. Thorleif Kimbi called out to Snorri, urging him to go after Steinthor and not let any of them get away alive. Snorri went over to the spot where Bergthor had been lying and saw a large clot of blood. He picked up a lump of snow mixed with blood, squeezed it, and put it up to his mouth. Then he asked whose blood it was, and Thorleif Kimbi said it was Bergthor who'd been bleeding. Snorri said this was blood from an internal wound.

'You're probably right,' said Thorleif. 'He was hit by a spear.'

'As far as I can judge,' said Snorri, 'it's a dying man's blood, so we needn't go after them.'

They carried the Thorbrandssons over to Helgafell, where their wounds were seen to. Thorodd Thorbrandsson had a deep cut on his neck and couldn't hold his head straight. He was wearing tight-fitting breeches, and they were soaked with blood. One of Snorri's men tried to help him undress, but no matter how hard he tugged, he couldn't get the breeches off.

'They're not exaggerating when they talk about your taste in clothes,' said the man. 'You Thorbrandssons wear such a tight fit they won't come off.'

'Then you can't be pulling hard enough,' said Thorodd.

The man braced his feet against the bench and gave another tug at the breeches as hard as he could, but still they wouldn't come off. Then Snorri the Priest came up and felt the leg, and saw that a spear was stuck right through it between the tendon and the shin-bone, skewering the trousers to the leg. Snorri said the man was remarkably stupid not to have noticed it.

Snorri Thorbrandsson was the fittest of the brothers, and in the evening he sat down at table with Snorri the Priest. There was cheese and curds for supper. Snorri the Priest thought his name-sake wasn't doing justice to the cheese, and asked why he was eating so slowly. Snorri Thorbrandsson said lambs were usually poor eaters when they'd just been gagged for weaning. Snorri the Priest felt his throat and found an arrow sticking right through at the base of the tongue. He got a pair of pincers and pulled it out, after which Snorri Thorbrandsson could take his food again.

Snorri the Priest was able to heal all the Thorbrandssons' wounds. When Thorodd's neck began to heal, his head tilted a bit, and he said Snorri was turning him into a cripple, but Snorri said he was sure the neck would straighten up once the sinews began to knit. Thorodd wanted to have the wound re-opened and the head set straighter, but it turned out just as Snorri had said it would, and once the sinews knit, Thorodd's head straightened up. All the same, Thorodd still found it hard to bend his head even a little.

Thorleif Kimbi walked with a wooden leg for the rest of his life.

CHAPTER 46

Settlement

STEINTHOR OF EYR AND HIS MEN ROWED to the boat-shed at Bakki and hauled the boat ashore. Two of the brothers were able to walk up to the farmstead, but they had to leave Bergthor behind and kept him there overnight in a tent. The story goes that Thormod's wife, Thorgerd, wouldn't go to bed with her husband that evening, but then someone came up from the boat-shed and told them Bergthor was dead. When Thorgerd heard this she went to bed as usual, and from what people say, there's no mention of any further disagreement between her and her husband. Steinthor went back home to Eyr in the morning, and for the rest of the winter things stayed quiet in the district.

In the spring, as Summons Days were drawing nearer, people of goodwill thought it a terrible thing if such great and close neighbours were to remain enemies and keep fighting one another; and so good men, friendly to both sides, tried to bring about a settlement between them. Vermund the Slender acted as spokesman, and had the backing of a number of good-natured people related to both parties. Eventually a truce was arranged between them, and then they were reconciled. Most people agree it was Vermund who acted as arbitrator and announced the verdict at the Thor's Ness Assembly with all the wisest men at his side. According to the terms of the settlement, the killings and assaults on both sides were paired off. It was agreed that the wound Thord Blig got at Alfta Fjord should cancel the one given to Thorodd Snorrason. Mar Hallvardsson's wound and the blow Steinthor gave Snorri the Priest were said to equal the deaths of the three men killed at Alfta Fjord. The killings by Styr, one on either side, cancelled each other out, as did the killing of Bergthor and the wounds of the Thorbrandssons in the fight on Vigra Fjord. The killing of Freystein Bofi was set against the killing of one of Steinthor's men at Alfta Fjord. Thorleif Kimbi got compensation for the leg he had lost. The killing of one of Snorri's men at Alfta

Fjord was matched against the unlawful assault Thorleif Kimbi had committed by starting the fight. All other injuries were evened out, all outstanding differences paid for, and so they parted on friendly terms. Everyone honoured this settlement as long as Steinthor and Snorri were both alive.

CHAPTER 47

Attempt on Bjorn's life

THAT SAME SUMMER, after the settlement, Thorodd the Tribute-Trader invited his brother-in-law Snorri the Priest to a feast at Frodriver, and Snorri came with eight companions. During the feast Thorodd complained to him about the shame and humiliation he'd suffered from Bjorn Asbrandsson's visits to his wife Thurid, Snorri's sister. Thorodd said he thought it Snorri's duty to put a stop to this embarrassing business. Snorri was at the feast for several days, and Thorodd gave him some fine gifts when they parted. From there Snorri rode south across the moor, saying he was on his way to the ship at Hraunhaven Mouth. This was during the hay-making season.

When they came south to Kamb Moor, Snorri said, 'Now we're going to ride down from the moor to Kamb, and I want you to know what I've decided. We're going to attack Bjorn and kill him if we can. But there aren't enough of us to get him in his own house – it's too well built, and he's a tough and courageous man. People have always found it hard to beat a powerful man like him when he's inside a house, even when they'd a much stronger force than we have. Take the case of Geir the Priest and Gizur the

White, when eighty of them attacked Gunnar of Hlidarend at his own house. Though he was fighting alone, he killed some of them and wounded others, and they'd have given up the attack if Geir the Priest hadn't been clever enough to see that Gunnar was running out of shot.[1] Now if Bjorn should be out of doors, as you'd expect in such fine drying weather, I want you to go after him, Mar; but take great care, Bjorn isn't a man to be trifled with, and unless we deal him his death-blow very quickly, you can expect a hard fight from that killer-wolf.'

They made their way down from the moor and rode straight to the farmstead, and there they saw Bjorn in the home-meadow making a hay-sled. He was on his own, with no weapons except a small adze and a big knife he was using to widen the mortises in the runners. The knife-blade was a span long.

Bjorn watched the riders coming down from the moor into the meadow, and recognised them at once. Snorri the Priest was in the lead wearing a blue cloak. Then Bjorn made a daring move. He picked up the knife and walked straight up to them. When he got to Snorri, he took hold of his cloak-sleeve with one hand and pointed the knife right at Snorri's chest with the other, ready to drive it home at once. Bjorn greeted them, and Snorri returned his greeting, but Mar lost his nerve when he saw how easily Bjorn could stab Snorri if anyone tried to rush him. Bjorn walked them on their way and asked the news, but he didn't relax the firm grip he had on Snorri.

'So it's come to this, Snorri,' said Bjorn. 'I can't deny it, I've done things to offend you, and you have good reason to hold them

---

1. An allusion to Gunnar's heroic last fight, described in *Njal's Saga*, tr. Magnusson & Pálsson, pp. 169–71.

against me. I've heard of the grudge you bear me, and I want you to tell me now whether you're here for a purpose or just passing by. If you want to see me, you'd better tell me why, otherwise give your word to leave me in peace, and I'll go back home. Nobody's going to make a fool of me.'

'This meeting of ours has turned out so well for you,' said Snorri, 'that I'll have to spare your life, no matter what I had in mind before we met. But I want to ask you to stop fooling around with my sister Thurid. We'll never be on good terms while you carry on like this.'

'I'll not promise you anything I can't carry out,' said Bjorn, 'and I'm not so sure that this is a promise I can honour while I'm living in the same neighbourhood as Thurid.'

'There's not much to keep you here,' said Snorri, 'you can easily leave the district.'

'You're right,' said Bjorn, 'and since you've come to see me about it, I'll do what you suggest. Our meeting is over now, but I promise you this: neither Thorodd nor yourself will be shamed by my visits in the future.'

'That's wise of you,' said Snorri.

With that they parted. Snorri rode on to the ship, and from there back home to Helgafell.

Next day Bjorn rode south to the ship at Hraun Haven and that same summer took his passage abroad. They were late putting out and ran into north-easterly gales which blew for a good part of the summer. Nothing was heard of the ship for a long time.

CHAPTER 48

To Greenland

WHEN THE PEACE-TERMS between the men of Eyr and those of Alftafjord had been arranged, Snorri Thorbrandsson and his brother Thorleif Kimbi sailed to Greenland. Thorleif lived there till he was an old man, and Kimba Bay between the glaciers in Greenland is named after him. Snorri went to Vinland the Good with Karlsefni and in a battle with the Skrælings[1] he died, a very brave man.

Thorodd Thorbrandsson took over the farm at Alftafjord. He married Ragnhild, daughter of Thord, son of Thorgils Eagle, son of Hallstein the Priest of Hallstein's Ness, who owned the slaves.[2]

CHAPTER 49

Christianity in Iceland

THE NEXT PART OF THE STORY TELLS how Gizur the White and his son-in-law Hjalti came to Iceland to preach the faith. Everyone in Iceland was baptised, and Christianity was adopted by law at the Althing. It was Snorri the Priest who more than anyone else persuaded the people in the Westfjords to embrace

---

1. *Skraeling* was the Icelandic word used to denote an indigenous inhabitant of Greenland or America: see *The Vinland Sagas*, tr. Magnusson & Pálsson.   2. An allusion to the *Book of Settlements*, Ch. 123.

the new faith. Soon after the Assembly broke up he started building a church at Helgafell, and his father-in-law Styr another one at Hraun. The priests promised each farmer as many places in Heaven as there was standing room in any church he might build, and this proved a great inducement to them to put up churches. Thorodd the Tribute-Trader had one built on his farm at Frodriver. But since there were only a few priests in Iceland at the time, it was hard to find any to sing mass in them.[1]

CHAPTER 50

Thorgunna

I N THE SUMMER THAT CHRISTIANITY WAS ADOPTED by law in Iceland, a ship from Dublin put in at Snæfell Ness. Most of the crew came from Ireland and the Hebrides, but there were some Norwegians too. They lay at Rif for a good part of the summer, then they got a fair wind to sail up the fjord to Dogurdar Ness, and a number of people from the neighbourhood came to trade with them there.

There was a Hebridean woman on board called Thorgunna, and the crew said she had some valuable things with her, very hard to get in Iceland. When Thurid of Frodriver heard about it, she very much wanted to see all this finery, for she was a vain woman and

---

1. The most detailed account of Iceland's conversion to Christianity is to be found in *Kristni Saga*. See also *Njal's Saga*, tr. Magnusson & Pálsson, pp. 216–24.

very fond of elegant clothes and adornment. She travelled to the ship to see Thorgunna and asked if she had something very special in ladies' clothing. Thorgunna said she had nothing for sale, but added that she had plenty of fine things to wear herself, so that she needn't be ashamed to go to feasts and other gatherings. Thurid asked her to show her the clothes, which Thorgunna did, and Thurid thought they were quite attractive and tastefully made, but not particularly expensive. Thurid offered to buy them, but Thorgunna wouldn't sell. Then Thurid invited her to come and stay with her, for she kept thinking about all the fine things she had seen, and hoping she could get them from her later on.

'Yes, I'd like to stay with you,' said Thorgunna. 'But there's something you should know. I'm not all that keen to pay for my board and lodging. I'm still a strong woman, and I don't mind working as long as I don't have to do anything rough. But I'll decide for myself how much of my own money I pay out.'

Thorgunna spoke very stiffly, but that didn't stop Thurid from urging her to come and stay with her; so Thorgunna had her baggage put ashore, a heavy trunk which she kept locked, and a lighter one, and both were taken to Frodriver. As soon as she got there, she asked to be shown to her bed, and she was given a place in the inner part of the main room. She opened the big chest and from it she took a set of bed-clothes, beautifully made. She spread English sheets on her bed, and laid a silk-covered quilt on top. She took bed-curtains from the chest and a canopy as well, and it all seemed so marvellous, no-one could remember having ever seen anything like it.

'How much would you take for the whole set?' asked Thurid.

'I don't care how refined and elegant you are,' said Thorgunna, 'I'm not going to sleep on bare straw just to please you.'

Thurid didn't like this at all, and that was the last time she offered to buy Thorgunna's things from her.

Thorgunna spent every day weaving, unless there was hay-making to do; and when the weather was good, she used to work at drying the hay in the home meadow. She had a special rake made for her and wouldn't let anyone else touch it. Thorgunna was a massive woman, tall, broadly-built, and getting very stout. She had dark eyebrows and narrow eyes, and beautiful chestnut hair. Her manner was always very proper, and she used to go to mass every morning before starting work, but she wasn't easy to get on with and didn't waste much time on conversation. People thought she must be in her fifties, though she was still a very active woman.

By this time Thorir Wood-Leg and his wife Thorgrima Witch-Face had come to live at Frodriver, and it wasn't long before there was trouble between them and Thorgunna. Kjartan the farmer's son was the only one there Thorgunna took to, and she liked him a lot: but he kept his distance, which she used to find very irritating. Kjartan was fourteen or fifteen at the time, a big lad, and very manly.

CHAPTER 51

Thorgunna dies

IT WAS A WET SUMMER, but there were good drying spells in the autumn once the home meadow at Frodriver had been mown, and nearly half of that hay was fully dry. Then there came a beautiful day, calm and clear, with not a cloud in sight. Thorodd

was up early that morning and arranged the work for the day;
some of the farmhands were to cart the hay home and others to
stack it. He told the women to help with the drying of the hay,
and shared out the work between them. Thorgunna was given as
much hay to dry as would have been winter fodder for an ox.

Everything went smoothly to begin with, but in the early
afternoon a black cloud began to form in the north, just above
Skor, and soon it swept across the sky, making straight for the
farmstead. It looked as if the cloud would bring rain, and Thorodd
told them to start stacking the hay, but Thorgunna kept turning
hers as hard as she could, and wouldn't begin to stack it even after
she'd been told to. The dark cloud raced across the sky, and when
it was just over the farmstead at Frodriver, it brought with it so
much darkness that they couldn't see anything beyond the
meadow, and hardly an arm's length inside it. After that there was
such a heavy cloudburst that all the hay on the ground was
drenched. The cloud vanished suddenly, and when the weather
cleared up again, they saw that the shower had been one of blood.

In the evening there was a fine drying-spell, and the blood
dried quickly, except on the hay that Thorgunna had spread.
There it wouldn't dry, nor would the rake she'd used.

Thorodd asked Thorgunna what this omen could mean, but she
said she couldn't tell. 'Most likely it forebodes the death of
someone here,' she said.

Thorgunna went home in the evening and straight to bed. She
took off the blood-soaked clothes she was wearing, lay down on
the bed and gave a heavy sigh. People realised that she must have
been taken ill. The shower hadn't fallen anywhere else, only on
Frodriver. Thorgunna wouldn't eat that evening. Next morning
Thorodd went to see her about her illness and ask when she thought

she'd be feeling better. She said she believed this illness would be her last.

'I've found you the most sensible person here,' she said, 'and that's why I'm telling you what to do with the things I leave behind. You may not think much of me, but everything I tell you will turn out exactly as I say, and nothing good will come of it if you don't follow my wishes. This first omen is a clear indication that something serious is bound to happen unless every necessary step is taken to prevent it.'

'You're probably not far from the truth,' said Thorodd. 'I promise to follow all your instructions.'

'Here's what I want,' said Thorgunna. 'Should I die of this illness I want my body taken to Skalholt, because something tells me it will soon become the most venerated place in the land.[1] I know there are priests there to sing Mass for me as well, and that's why I want you to take me there. In return you can have enough of my belongings to reward you handsomely for all your trouble. But before you start dividing up my things, Thurid is to have the scarlet cloak. I'm doing this to make her less unhappy about the arrangements for the rest of my things. Next take enough to cover your expenses on my account, whatever you and your wife would most like to have out of all the things I'm leaving with you. There's a gold ring that must go with me, and that's to be given to the church: but my bed and all its furnishings I want burnt to ashes, for they'll never do anyone much good. I'm not saying this because I grudge these things to anyone who could use them, but

---

1. In 1056 Skalholt became the seat of the first native Icelandic bishop; and soon it was an important centre of learning and culture. It remained an episcopal see until the end of the eighteenth century.

I must be firm about it, as I wouldn't like to be responsible for all the trouble people will bring on themselves if they don't respect my wishes.'

Thorodd promised to do all that she'd asked him. Soon after, her illness took a turn for the worse and she didn't have to wait many days before she died.

The body was taken to church and Thorodd had a coffin made for it. Next day he carried the bedclothes outside, gathered some firewood, and made a bonfire. When his wife Thurid came and asked what he was up to, he said he was going to burn them, just as Thorgunna had asked.

'You're not burning valuable things like these, if I have my way,' she said.

'She meant every word when she said it wouldn't do to ignore her warning,' said Thorodd.

'It only goes to show what an envious woman she was,' said Thurid. 'She was too mean to let anyone else enjoy them, and that's why she told you to do it. No matter what we decide to do, I can't see what harm can come of it.'

'I don't think ignoring her wishes will do us much good,' he said.

But then Thurid put her arms round his neck and begged him not to burn the bed-furnishings. She kept pleading with him until he agreed that he'd only destroy the eiderdown and pillows, while Thurid took the quilt, the bed-curtains, and the canopy. All the same, neither of them felt really happy about it.

Then they got ready to send the corpse off for burial. For the journey Thorodd chose men he could rely on and gave them his best horses. The corpse was wrapped in an unstitched linen shroud and laid in a coffin. They set off, taking the usual route south across the moor, and there's nothing particular to say of their journey till they came south of Valbjarnarvellir. As they crossed the sodden moorland there, the pack-horse kept throwing off the coffin. On they went, south to the Nordur River, and crossed it at Eyjar Ford through very deep water. The weather was squally with sleet and heavy rain. Eventually they came to a farm called Nether Ness in Stafholfstungur and asked to stay the night, but the farmer wouldn't give them any hospitality. It was getting very late, and they thought they couldn't travel any further, because it didn't seem wise to risk fording the Hvit River at night. So they unloaded their horses, carried the coffin into a store-house near the door, walked into the living-room, and took off their clothes, intending to spend the night there without any food if necessary.

The household went to bed before it grew dark. They hadn't been long in their beds when they heard loud noises coming from the larder. Some of them went to see if thieves had broken into the house; and when they came to the larder, there was a tall woman, stark-naked, not a stitch of clothing on her, getting a meal ready. When they saw her, the people of the household were too scared to come anywhere near her. As soon as the corpse-bearers knew about it, they went to see for themselves what was going on. The woman there was Thorgunna, and everyone thought it best to leave her in peace. When she'd finished doing what she wanted in the larder, she carried the food into the living-room, laid the table, and served the meal.

'You may end up very sorry before we part that you didn't treat us more hospitably,' said the corpse-bearers to the farmer.

'We'll gladly give you food and anything else you need,' said the farmer and his wife.

And as soon as the farmer had made them welcome, Thorgunna walked out of the room and didn't reappear.

Now a lamp was lit in the living-room, and the travellers were helped out of their wet clothes and given dry things. They sat down at table and made the sign of the cross over the food, and the farmer had every corner of the house sprinkled with holy water. The travellers ate their food, and it didn't harm them in the least, even though it had been prepared by Thorgunna. They spent a very comfortable night there.

In the morning they got ready to be on their way, and the rest of the journey went without a hitch. Everyone who heard what had happened at the first farm thought it best to give them all that they asked for, and nothing else happened on the journey. They came to Skalholt and handed over the valuable gifts Thorgunna had left for the church there, which the priests accepted with pleasure. So Thorgunna was buried, and the corpse-bearers set off home. They had an easy journey and got back safely.

CHAPTER 52

An omen

THE FARM AT FRODRIVER had a large living-room with a bed-closet behind it, as was usual in those days. In front of the living-room there were two store-rooms on either side of the door, one for dried fish and the other for flour. They used to have a great fire burning in the living-room every evening, and people used to sit beside it for hours on end before they had their evening meal.

The same evening as the corpse-bearers came back, the people at Frodriver were sitting by the fireside when they saw a half-moon appear on the panelled wall. Everyone could see it. The moon kept circling round the room, backing from left to right, and it didn't disappear as long as the people remained at the fire.

Thorodd asked Thorir Wood-Leg what it meant, and Thorir said it was a fatal moon. 'There'll be deaths here,' he added.

It went on like this for a whole week; every evening the same weird moon appeared in the living-room.

CHAPTER 53

The hauntings begin

THE NEXT THING TO HAPPEN WAS that the shepherd came home one day, badly shaken. He didn't say much; and when he did speak, he was very rough-tempered. He fought shy of other people and kept muttering to himself, so everyone thought he must have been bewitched. This went on for some time. When two weeks of winter had passed, he came home one evening, went straight to bed and lay down. Next morning, when people went to see him they found him dead. He was buried at the church there, and not long afterwards massive hauntings began at the place.

One night Thorir Wood-Leg went out to the privy to ease himself, and when he was on his way back to the house, he saw the shepherd standing in front of the door. Thorir tried to get inside, but the shepherd barred his way. Thorir started walking away, but the shepherd came after him, picked him up, and threw him hard against the door. This gave Thorir a nasty shock and a good many bruises, but he struggled back to bed. Later he became ill, then died, and was buried at the church there. After that, the pair of them, Thorir Wood-Leg and the shepherd, were often seen together. As was only natural, people were terrified.

After Thorir's death, one of Thorodd's farmhands fell ill. He lay in bed for three days, and then he died. Soon people started dying one after another, six of them in all. This was just about the beginning of Advent, but in those days people in Iceland didn't observe the fast, and the store-room was stacked so full with dried fish that the door would hardly open. The pile of fish went right up to the cross-beam, and people had to use a ladder to get at it from above. Then things started happening. Night after night, as people were sitting at the fire, they could hear something tearing at the dried fish, but when they went to look they couldn't see a living thing there.

That winter, shortly before Christmas, Thorodd went out to Ness to get more dried fish for himself. There were six of them together in a ten-oared boat, and they spent the night at Ness. In the evening, after Thorodd had gone and the fire had been lit, the people came into the living-room and saw a seal's head coming up through the floor. One of the servants was the first to notice this as she came in, and she grabbed a club in the doorway and hit the seal on the head. This only made the seal rise up a bit more out of the ground. Then it turned its eyes towards the canopy from Thorgunna's bed. One of the farmhands came up and started hitting the seal, but it kept rising further up with every blow, until its flippers emerged. At that the man fainted, and everyone was paralysed with horror, except for young Kjartan, who rushed up with a sledge-hammer and struck the seal on the head. It was a powerful blow, but the seal only shook its head and gazed around. Kjartan went on hammering the head and driving it down like a nail into the floor till the seal disappeared into it, then he flattened out the floor above its head. Throughout the winter it was always the same story, Kjartan was the only one who could put fear into the ghosts.

CHAPTER 54

More ghosts

NEXT MORNING Thorodd and his men put out from Ness with their dried fish, and they were all drowned off Enni. The boat and the fish were washed ashore there, but the bodies were never found.

When the news came to Frodriver, Kjartan and Thurid invited their neighbours to a funeral feast, at which they used the Christmas ale. On the first evening of the feast, when all the guests were seated, Thorodd and his companions came into the room drenched to the skin. Everyone welcomed Thorodd and his men, and thought this a happy omen, because in those days it was believed that drowned people had been well received by Ran, goddess of the sea, if they came to their own funeral feast. At that time a good many heathen beliefs still prevailed, though people were baptised and supposed to be Christians. Thorodd and his men walked across the main room, which had two doors, and into the living-room. They ignored the greetings people gave them and sat down at the fire. The people bolted out of the living-room, but Thorodd and his men stayed on until the fire began to burn very low, then went away. This went on as long as the funeral feast lasted – every evening the drowned men would come to the fire. It gave people at the feast plenty to talk about, but some of them thought it would all stop once the feast was over.

After the feast, all the guests went back home, and the place seemed rather dull without them. In the evening after the guests had gone the fire in the living-room was lit as usual, and as soon as it was ablaze, Thorodd and his companions came in, all of them soaking wet. They sat down at the fire and began squeezing the water out of their clothes. No sooner had they taken their seats than Thorir Wood-Leg and his six companions came into the room, all of them covered with earth. They started shaking the dirt out of their clothes and throwing mud at Thorodd and his men. The people bolted out of the room, as you'd expect, and that evening they had to do without light, heating-stones, and everything else the fire could give.[1] Next evening they lit a fire in another room, hoping the dead men wouldn't come there, but things didn't turn out that way – everything happened just as before, and both parties came to sit by the fire. On the third evening, Kjartan suggested they should light a long-fire[2] in the living room, and another in a separate room for the household, so they tried that. As it turned out, Thorodd and the other dead men came and sat at the long-fire, while the living sat at the smaller one. This was how it went throughout the Christmas season.

By that time the noises from the fish-pile had grown much louder, and day and night people could hear the fish being torn up. Soon the time came for the fish to be eaten, and they had a look at the pile. Someone got on top of it and saw a tail sticking out of the pile. It had the look of a singed ox-tail, but it was covered with short seal-hair. The man on the stack got hold of it. First he tried

---

1. Stones were heated by the fire and then used to warm up food and drinks. 2. *Langeldr*, a long hearth running down the centre of the main room. See *Njal's Saga*, tr. Magnusson & Pálsson, p. 55.

to pull it out himself, then called for others to come and help him. Several people, men and women, joined him on the stack and kept pulling at the tail, but they couldn't budge it an inch. Everybody thought the tail was dead, but as they were struggling to get it out, the tail tore right through their hands, and the skin was ripped off the palms of those who'd been pulling hardest. The tail was never seen again. They started clearing the fish out of the store-room, and when they got down into the pile, they saw that all the meat had been torn off the fish and only the skins left behind. But there wasn't a living creature in it anywhere.

Shortly afterwards Thorgrima Witch-Face, Thorir Wood-Leg's widow, fell ill, and after a short spell in bed she died. On the very evening of her burial she was seen in her husband's company. Then the sickness that had been raging when the hairy tail had made its first appearance broke out again, this time killing more women than men. Six people died one after another, and the hauntings and night-walkings drove others away from the farm. There had been thirty servants there in the autumn, but eighteen of them died, five more ran away, and by mid-winter there were only seven of them left.

CHAPTER 55

The ghosts are banished

AFTER THESE WEIRD HAPPENINGS had been going on for some time, Kjartan set off one day over to Helgafell to see his uncle Snorri and ask his advice about what should be done to put an end to them. At that time there was a priest staying at Helgafell, sent to Snorri by Gizur the White. Snorri asked the priest to go with Kjartan to Frodriver along with his son Thord the Cat and six other people. They must burn the canopy from Thorgunna's bed, said Snorri, and then summons all the dead men to a door-court. After that the priest was to sing mass, consecrate water, and hear people's confessions. They rode over to Frodriver, and on the way there they asked the neighbours to come with them.

It was Candlemas Eve when they came to Frodriver, and the fire had just been lit. Thurid had been taken with the same illness as those who had died. Kjartan went straight into the living-room and saw Thorodd and the other dead people sitting at the fire as usual. He pulled down the canopy from Thorgunna's bed, plucked a brand from the fire, went out, and burnt to ashes all the bed-furnishings that had once belonged to Thorgunna.

Then Kjartan summonsed Thorir Wood-Leg, and Thord the Cat summonsed Thorodd for trespassing on the home and robbing people of life and health. All the dead ones at the fire were summonsed in the same way. Then the door-court was held and charges made, the proper procedure of ordinary law-courts being observed throughout. The jury was appointed, testimony was taken, and the cases were summed up and referred to judgment. When sentence was being passed on Thorir Wood-Leg, he rose to his feet and said, 'I've sat here as long as people would let me.' Then he went out through the door at which the court was not being held.

After that, sentence was passed on the shepherd, and he stood up. 'I'll go now, and it seems I should have gone sooner,' he said.

When Thorgrima Witch-Face heard her sentence, she stood up, too. 'I've stayed as long as you've let me,' she said.

So they all received their sentences one after another; and each, on being sentenced, got up, made some such remark, and left the room. It was clear that none of them wanted to go.

Thorodd was the last to be sentenced. When he heard the judgment, he stood up. 'There's no peace here,' he said, 'we'd best all be on our way.' And with that he walked out.

Then Kjartan and the others went back inside, and the priest carried holy water and sacred relics to every corner of the house. Next day he sang all the prayers and celebrated mass with great solemnity, and there were no more dead men haunting Frodriver after that. Thurid began to improve and got well again. In the spring after all these strange happenings Kjartan engaged new servants. He farmed at Frodriver for a long time, and people thought him a very brave man.

CHAPTER 56

Snorri's enemies

SNORRI THE PRIEST LIVED at Helgafell for eight years after Christianity was adopted by law in Iceland. During Snorri's last year at Helgafell, his father-in-law, Styr, was killed at Jorvi in Flisuhverfi, and he travelled south to Hrossholt to fetch Styr's body. When he came into the women's room, there was Styr sitting up with his arms round the farmer's daughter.

In the spring Snorri exchanged farms with Gudrun, Osvif's

Daughter, and moved house to Tongue in Sælingsdale, two years after Gudrun's husband Bolli Thorleiksson had been killed.[1]

That same spring Snorri and his men went south to Borgarfjord, four hundred strong, to take action over the killing of Styr. With him were Styr's brother, Vermund the Slender, living then at Vatnsfjord, Steinthor of Eyr, Thorodd Thorbrandsson of Alfta-fjord, Styr's nephew, Thorleik Brandsson of Kross Ness, and a good many other important men. But they could only go as far as the Hvit River to Haug's Ford across the river from Bæ, because waiting for them on the south bank were Illugi the Black, Kleppjarn the Old, Thorstein Gislason, Gunnlaug Adder-Tongue, Thorstein Thorgilsson of Hafursfjord Island, who was married to Vigdis, Illugi the Black's daughter, and many other notable men, more than five hundred strong.

Since Snorri and his men were barred from crossing the river, they started proceedings when they had got as close to the others as they thought safe. Snorri summonsed Gest for the killing of Styr, but that summer at the Althing Thorstein Gislason dismissed Snorri's case. In the autumn Snorri rode south to Borgarfjord and killed Thorstein Gislason and his son Gunnar. Along with Snorri on that expedition there were fifteen men all told, among them Steinthor of Eyr, Thorodd Thorbrandsson, Bard Hoskuldsson, and Thorleik Brandsson.

Next spring Snorri the Priest and Thorstein of Hafursfjord Island, Illugi the Black's son-in-law, met at the Thor's Ness

---

1. An allusion to *Laxdæla Saga*. Gudrun egged her husband Bolli on into killing Kjartan, his cousin and blood-brother, and later Kjartan's brothers took revenge and killed Bolli. Snorri seems to have moved to Tongue in 1008.

Assembly. (Thorstein was the son of Thorgils, son of Thorfinn, son of Sel-Thorir of Raudamel. Thorstein's mother was Aud, daughter of Alf of the Dales, so Thorstein was cousin to Thorgils Arason of Reykjahills, Thorgeir Havarsson, and Thorgils Holluson, as well as to the men of Alftafjord, Thorleif Kimbi and the other Thorbrandssons.) Thorstein had prepared a number of law-suits for the Assembly, and one day, on the slope near the court, Snorri asked Thorstein if he had many law-suits this time. Thorstein said he had several.

'I daresay you'd like us to be as helpful to you with your cases as you and the men of Borgarfjord were to me last summer?' asked Snorri.

'No, I don't think I would,' said Thorstein.

After this, Snorri's sons and Styr's kinsmen had a good many harsh words for Thorstein, saying that it would serve him right if all his cases were dismissed and that he deserved to pay with his life for all the humiliation he and his father-in-law Illugi had caused them the previous summer. Thorstein didn't bother to answer, and people went away.

Thorstein and his kinsmen from Raudamel had a large force, and when the court was in session he hoped to push through all the cases he had brought. Styr's kinsmen got to hear about it, and armed themselves to keep the men of Raudamel from the court by force, should they try to approach it. This led to a pitched battle between them. Thorstein of Hafursfjord Island had only one thought in mind, to get at Snorri the Priest. Thorstein was tall and strong, and a great fighting-man. But as Thorstein was forcing his way towards Snorri, Snorri's nephew, Kjartan of Frodriver, raced up to defend him. Kjartan and Thorstein set on one another, and the fight was long and hard before friends on both sides came between them and arranged a truce.

After the battle, Snorri the Priest said to his nephew Kjartan, 'Plenty of fighting today, Breidaviking!'[2]

Kjartan was furious. 'Don't blame me for my background,' he said.

Thorstein lost seven men in the battle, and a number were wounded on both sides, but the quarrel was settled on the spot at the Assembly, and Snorri's terms were very generous. He didn't want this case to come to the Althing, for no settlement had been reached over the killing of Thorstein Gislason, and he knew he would have quite enough on his hands without having to cope with yet another case.

Thormod Trefilsson described these events, the killing of Thorstein Gislason and his son Gunnar, and the Battle of the Thor's Ness Assembly, in his *Lay of the Raven*:

> *Two men were slain*
> *by the brave soldier;*
> *swords rang*
> *south of the river;*
> *robbed of their lives*
> *seven more dead*
> *slept at Thor's Ness*
> *for all men to see.*

It was part of their agreement that Thorstein should be free to bring all the actions he had referred to the Thor's Ness Assembly. And at the Althing that same summer, a settlement was made over

---

2. An allusion to Kjartan's paternity: he was the son of Thorodd and Thurid, but his real father was thought to be Bjorn. See p. 129.

the killing of Thorstein Gislason and his son Gunnar. Those who had taken part with Snorri in these killings agreed to go abroad.

In the summer Thorstein of Hafursfjord Island withdrew the chieftaincy of Raudamel from the Thor's Ness Assembly as he didn't like the way Snorri and his supporters seemed to have got the better of him. After that Thorstein and his kinsmen set up an assembly at Straumfjord, which survived for quite a long time.3

CHAPTER 57

Ospak

WHILE SNORRI HAD BEEN FARMING at Tongue in Sælings-dale Tongue for some years, a man called Ospak was living to the north at Eyr in Bitra. Ospak was the son of Kjallak of Kjallak's River near Skridinsenni, and was married, with a son called Glum, still a young man. Ospak was big and strong, but he was also a great bully, and nobody liked him. He used to go about with seven or eight men, all guilty of different offences against the farmers there in the north. Glum and his men used to sail near the coast, robbing the farmers of anything they wanted and stealing their driftwood.1

---

3. According to the ancient Icelandic constitution, each local assembly (there were 13 of them for the whole country) was supported by three chieftains. Nothing is known about the Straumfjord Assembly mentioned here.

---

1. Driftage rights were considered a great asset to coastal farmers. Meat from stranded whales was a welcome addition to the larder, and driftwood was widely used for building.

There was a man called Alf the Short at Thambardale in Bitra, well-off, and running a good farm. Alf was one of Snorri's supporters and looked after his driftage rights on Gudlaug's Head. Like so many other farmers, Alf had plenty of grievances against Ospak and his men, and used to complain about them every time he saw Snorri.

At that time Thorir Gull-Hardarson was farming at Tongue in Bitra. He was a friend of Killer Sturla Thjodreksson who lived at Stadarhol in Saurbæ. Thorir was a thrifty farmer and the leading man of Bitra. He looked after Sturla's driftage rights there in the north. Ospak and Thorir were always at loggerheads, and sometimes one and then the other would come out on top. Ospak was the most important farmer in the districts of Krossardale and Enni.

One year winter set in early with heavy frost and snow, so there was no grazing in Bitra. The farmers suffered great losses in livestock, but some of them managed to get their herds south over the moor. The previous summer, Ospak had fortified the farmstead at Eyr, turning it into a powerful stronghold. Just after midwinter a fierce blizzard blew up from the north, and lasted for a week. When the weather cleared, people saw there was drift ice out in the bay, but it hadn't come into the fjord at Bitra. The farmers set out to scour the beaches for driftage, and soon the story went about that a big finback whale had come ashore between Stika and Gudlaug's Head. Snorri the Priest and Sturla Thjodreksson had the greatest claim to the whale, but Alf the Short and other farmers had a share in it too. Some of the Bitra people went with Thorir and Alf to cut up the whale, and as they were busy carving it up, they saw a boat coming from Eyr across the fjord. It wasn't long before they recognised the twelve-oared boat belonging to Ospak. The crew beached the boat near the whale and walked ashore, fifteen strong, and fully armed. Ospak made straight for the whale and asked who was in charge. Thorir said he was looking after Sturla's share and Alf was seeing to his and Snorri's. 'The other farmers are taking care of their own shares,' he added.

Ospak asked how much of the whale they were going to let him have.

'You won't get anything of what I'm responsible for,' said Thorir, 'but I can't speak for the other farmers. They may be willing to sell you theirs. How much do you want to pay for it?'

'You ought to know better, Thorir,' said Ospak. 'I'm not in the habit of buying whale-meat from you Bitra people.'

'I don't think you'll get any without paying for it,' said Thorir.

The chunks of whale-meat already cut were piled up in a heap, but they hadn't yet been shared out. Ospak told his men to start loading the meat into the boat. The whale-cutters had no weapons except for their meat-axes, but when Thorir saw Ospak and his men making for the whale, he told the farmers they oughtn't to put up with this robbery, and they all rushed forward, with Thorir in the lead. Ospak turned to meet him and struck Thorir with the back of his axe. The blow landed on his ear and knocked him senseless. The men with him pulled him back and tried to bring him round, so there was nobody left to defend the whale.

Then Alf the Short came forward and asked Ospak not to take the whale. 'You'd better keep out of this, Alf,' said Ospak, 'you have a thin skull, and I've got a heavy axe. One step more, and you'll finish up worse than Thorir.' It was good advice, and Alf took it.

Ospak and his men started loading the whale-meat into the boat and just as they'd finished, Thorir came to. He saw what had happened and spoke angrily to his men for being such cowards as to stand idly by, watching people being robbed and beaten. At that he sprang to his feet, but Ospak and his men had already launched his boat and put out to sea. They rowed across the fjord over to Eyr, and started work on what they'd stolen. Ospak wouldn't let anyone go away who'd been with him on this trip, so they all stayed on at the fortified farmstead, and got ready to withstand a siege.

Thorir and the others divided up what was left of the whale, each taking his proper share of the loss, and then they went back home. Thorir and Ospak were now bitter enemies. Ospak had a lot of men with him, and soon he began to run out of provisions.

CHAPTER 58

Fighting

ONE NIGHT OSPAK SET OUT with fourteen men and travelled to Thambardale. They went straight into the house, herded Alf and his household into the living-room, looted the farm and carried their plunder away on four horses. The people at Fjardarhorn saw them leaving and sent someone over to Tongue to tell Thorir. He quickly gathered some men and set out eighteen strong for the head of the fjord, where he saw Ospak and his men riding north from Fjardarhorn.

When Ospak saw riders following them, he said, 'There are some men over there. It must be Thorir out to avenge the blow I gave him earlier in the winter. There are eighteen of them against our fifteen, but we're better armed, and it's hard to say who is keener for a fight. The horses we took from Thambardale would

M 177

run back home, but I'm not going to give up what I've stolen. The two weakest here had better drive them over to Eyr and tell my men to hurry up and help us. The rest of us must stand here and fight, no matter what comes of it.' They did as he told them.

When Thorir came up with his men, Ospak greeted them and asked the news, talking very smoothly to gain time. Thorir asked where they'd gained all this loot, and Ospak said at Thambardale.

'How did you come by it?' asked Thorir.

'It wasn't given or sold,' said Ospak, 'and nothing was paid for it.'

'Will you let it go, and hand it over to us?' asked Thorir.

Ospak said he didn't much feel like doing so.

At that they set on one another and the fighting started. Thorir and his men moved hard into the attack, but Ospak's party defended strongly in spite of being outnumbered. Some were soon wounded and others killed. Thorir, armed with a barbed spear, charged up to Ospak and lunged at him with it, but he parried the blow. Thorir had put all his strength into it, and when he missed, he went down on his knees with his head touching the ground. Ospak hewed at him with the back of his axe and there was a loud crack.

'Maybe this will teach you not to take such long trips away from home, Thorir,' he said.

'You could be right,' said Thorir, 'but I don't think a knock from you is going to stop me making all the trips I want.' He'd been wearing a knife on a strap round his neck, as people used to in those days, and the knife happened to be dangling down his back. That was where the blow had landed, so he was only slightly wounded on either side of the knife.

One of Thorir's companions aimed a blow at Ospak, but he parried it with his axe. The sword struck the axe-handle and broke it in two, so that the axe-head fell to the ground. Then Ospak took to his heels and told his men to run for it. Thorir got back on to his feet and a spear-throw of his caught Ospak in the thigh and went straight through. Ospak pulled the spear out of the wound, turned round, hurled it at the man who'd first tried to strike him, and killed him instantly. Ospak and his companions ran off, and Thorir and his men chased them north along the beaches up to Eyr, where a number of people, men and women, came running down from the farm; so Thorir and his men had to turn back. There were no more clashes between them for the rest of the winter. Three of Ospak's men were killed in the fight, and one of Thorir's, but a good many were wounded on either side.

CHAPTER 59
More looting

SNORRI THE PRIEST TOOK OVER the case against Ospak and his men from Alf the Short, and had them all sentenced to outlawry at the Thor's Ness Assembly. When it was over, Snorri went back home to Tongue and waited till it was time to hold the court of confiscation.[1] Then he set off north to Bitra with a large

---

1. A convicted outlaw forfeited the right to own property, and a formal court of confiscation was supposed to be held over him at his home fourteen days after sentence had been passed. When the creditors had been paid what the outlaw owed and the chieftain had taken his fee for holding the court, the rest of the confiscated property was shared out between the judges and the farmers in the district.

number of men, but found that Ospak had gone, taking all his belongings with him. In fact Ospak had sailed off north to the Strands, with fifteen men in two boats, and there they stayed for the rest of the summer, causing plenty of trouble. They settled down at Tharalatursfjord in the north, and men began gathering round them. They were joined by a man called Hrafn the Viking a criminal who'd been living as an outlaw in the North Strands. They did a lot of damage in these parts with their looting and killing, and the whole gang of them stayed there till the beginning of winter. Then the men of the Strands got together, and with several other farmers Olaf Eyvindarson of Drangar led an attack on the outlaws, who had fortified the farm at Tharalatursfjord and were now thirty strong. Olaf and his men besieged the stronghold, but it seemed quite impregnable. The farmers talked things over with the trouble-makers, who offered to clear out of the Strands and not do any more harm there. Since the farmers thought they were never going to gain the upper hand, they accepted the offer, and both sides swore an oath to keep the agreement. After that the farmers went back home.

CHAPTER 60

Thorir is killed

As for Snorri the Priest, he set off north to Bitra to hold the court of confiscation and found that Ospak had gone away from Eyr. Snorri held the court of confiscation fully according to law, claimed the property of the outlaws, and divided it out between Alf the Short and all the other farmers who had suffered most through the outlaws' robberies. After that Snorri the Priest rode back home to Tongue.

The summer passed, and at the beginning of winter Ospak and his men left the North Strands in two large boats. They sailed south along the coast and then across the bay over to Vatns Ness, where they went ashore and loaded up two full cargoes of stolen goods. After that they sailed back west across the bay over to Bitra, put in at Eyr, and carried the loot into the fortified farmhouse. Ospak's wife and his son Glum had stayed behind with two cows.

That same night the outlaws put out again, sailed their two boats up to the head of the fjord, walked up to the farmstead at Tongue, and broke into the house. They dragged Thorir out of bed, led him outside, and killed him on the spot. They rifled the house, taking whatever they could lay their hands on, and carried everything down to the boats, then rowed over to Thambardale, rushed up to the farmstead, and broke the door down as they had done at Tongue. Alf the Short was in bed fully dressed, and when he heard the door coming down he ran out through a secret passage at the back of the house and got away into the valley.

Ospak and his men stole everything they could lay their hands on there and carried it down to the boats. They sailed back to Eyr with their boats fully loaded, and took all they'd stolen into the fortified farmhouse, then hauled the boats into the stronghold and filled them with water. They made the stronghold completely impregnable, and they stayed there throughout the winter.

CHAPTER 61

Alf and Snorri

ALF THE SHORT SET OFF RUNNING south across the moor
and didn't stop till he came to Tongue, where he told his troubles
to Snorri the Priest, trying to get him to set out north right away
and attack Ospak. But first Snorri wanted to get more news from
the north, to find out whether Ospak had done anything more than
scare Alf away, and whether he'd settled down somewhere else
in Bitra. A little later the news came south from Bitra that Ospak
had killed Thorir, and that it wasn't going to be easy to take his
stronghold.

Snorri sent for Alf's family, with what was left of his belongings,
and they stayed with him for the rest of the winter. Snorri's enemies
criticised him for being so slow in putting things right for Alf, but
he let people talk, and still did nothing. So Sturla Thjodreksson
sent word east to Snorri that he was ready to join him any time in
an attack on Ospak, saying it was just as much his duty as Snorri's.

Throughout the winter up to Christmas, reports kept coming
in from the north that Ospak and his men were causing trouble.
The weather was bitterly cold, with all the fjords frozen over.
Just before Lent, Snorri the Priest sent a messenger west to
Ingjaldshvall in Ness to a farmer there called Thrand Stigandi,
son of the Ingjald who gave his name to Ingjaldshvall. Thrand was
an exceptionally big and powerful man and a very fast runner.
At one time he'd been a member of Snorri's household. Thrand
was said to have been a sorcerer in his heathen days, but most
people gave up all their witchcraft once they were baptised. Snorri
sent word asking him to come east to Tongue and get ready for a

dangerous mission. When the message arrived, Thrand spoke to the messenger. 'Relax here as long as you like,' he said, 'I'm going to do what Snorri tells me, but you'll never be able to keep up with me.'

The messenger said he couldn't tell until they'd tried it, but in the morning, when he got up, Thrand had already gone and taken his weapons. Thrand walked east by Enni, then followed the usual path to Buland Head, round the heads of the fjords to the farm called Eid. From there he crossed Kolgrafa Fjord, Selja Fjord, and Vigra Fjord, then up to the head of Hvamm Fjord, all the way over the ice, and came to Tongue in the evening when Snorri was having his meal. He and Thrand greeted each other warmly, then Thrand asked what Snorri wanted of him and said he was ready to go anywhere, no matter what Snorri had in mind. Snorri asked him to stay the night and rest, and someone came to help Thrand off with his wet clothes.

CHAPTER 62

The criminals are killed

THAT SAME NIGHT SNORRI THE PRIEST sent another messenger west to Stadarhol to ask Sturla Thjodreksson to come and join him the following day at Tongue north in Bitra. Snorri sent for his neighbours, too, and next day they set out fifty strong north across Gafl Fell Moor. They came to Tongue in the evening, where Sturla was waiting for them with thirty men, and that night they went north to Eyr. When they got there, Ospak came out on to the stronghold wall and asked who was their leader. They

told him who they were, and ordered the men in the stronghold
to surrender. Ospak said he would never do that, 'But,' said he,
'we'll make you the same offer as we made to the men of the
Strands: we'll leave the district, if you'll go away from our stronghold.' Snorri said it wasn't for Ospak and his men to lay down
terms.

In the morning at daybreak they planned the assault on the
stronghold, dividing it between them. Snorri the Priest was to
attack the side defended by Hrafn the Viking, and Sturla was to
tackle Ospak's side. Sam and Bork, the sons of Bork the Stout,
were to attack the third side, and Snorri's sons Thorodd and
Thorstein the Cod-Biter the fourth. Mostly Ospak and his men
used stones to hold off the attack, but they fought well and kept up
a good steady stream of missiles. Snorri and Sturla hit back at
them with arrows and spears. They had a good supply, because
they had taken time over their preparations to make sure they'd
overcome the stronghold. There was fierce fighting, and several
men on both sides were wounded, but nobody was killed. Snorri
and his men kept up such a rain of weapons that Hrafn's party was
forced to take cover behind the wall. Then Thrand Stigandi took
a running jump and got high enough up the wall to hook his axe
over the top. He climbed up the shaft hand over fist, and made his
way into the stronghold. When Hrafn saw him coming he rushed
at him, lunging with a spear, but Thrand parried, then hewed at
Hrafn's shoulder and severed his arm. By that time there was a
crowd of them all round him, but he jumped off the wall and
managed to get back to the others.

Ospak kept urging his men to stand firm, and put up a brave
fight himself. He went right up to the wall to throw stones at
Sturla and his men, but once he went too far, and the thonged

spear which Sturla threw at Ospak caught him in the waist and knocked him right off the wall. Sturla rushed up and wouldn't let anyone else touch him, for he didn't want there to be any doubt that he was Ospak's killer. Soon a third man was killed, this time at the wall which Bork's sons were attacking.

Then the vikings surrendered, on condition they'd neither be killed nor maimed. They said they'd agree to any terms Snorri and Sturla wanted, and since the attackers were running out of missiles, they accepted the offer. So the men in the stronghold laid down their arms and surrendered to Snorri the Priest, and he honoured their condition that they'd be neither maimed nor killed. Hrafn, Ospak, and another man were dead, and there were plenty of wounded on both sides.

This is how Thormod Trefilsson describes the battle in his *Lay of the Raven*:

> *In the battle of Bitra*
> *the brisk fighter gave*
> *hungry birds of prey*
> *plenty of flesh to peck.*
> *Three savage vikings,*
> *sailors of many seas,*
> *lay fallen dead,*
> *food for the raven's feast.*

Snorri the Priest let Ospak's widow and their son Glum keep the farm there. Later, Glum married Thordis, daughter of Asmund Grey-Lock and sister of Grettir the Strong,[1] and their son was

---

1. The hero of *Grettir's Saga*.

Ospak, who quarrelled with Odd Ofeigsson of Midfjord.[2] Snorri
the Priest and Sturla drove all these vikings away, scattering them
in all directions, and, once having dealt with them, went back
home. Thrand Stigandi stayed with Snorri the Priest for a short
while, and they went back home to Ingjaldshvall. Snorri thanked
Stigandi handsomely for supporting him so well. Thrand Stigandi
farmed for a long time at Ingjaldshvall and later at Thrandstad.
He was a great man.

CHAPTER 63

Thorolf comes back from the dead

THORODD THORBRANDSSON WAS STILL FARMING at
Alftafjord, and owned the estates at Ulfarsfell and Orlygsstad
as well. Thorolf Twist-Foot's ghost kept haunting these farms so
violently that no-one would live there. Bolstad was now derelict,
for no sooner was Arnkel dead than Thorolf had begun to haunt
there too, killing men and beasts alike, so that no-one at that time
had the courage to farm there. After Bolstad was abandoned,
Thorolf moved over to Ulfarsfell, where he did a great deal of
damage. Everyone on the farm was terrified whenever Thorolf
appeared on the scene. The farmer at Ulfarsfell was Thorodd's
tenant, so he went to Karsstad to complain, saying that everyone

---

2. An allusion to *The Confederates* (*Bandamanna Saga*), one of the best
shorter sagas.

felt that unless something was done, Thorolf wouldn't stop until he'd cleared everything from the neighbourhood, men, beasts, and all. 'I can't stay there any longer unless something is done about it,' he said.

Thorodd listened to his tenant, but didn't know how to deal with the problem. In the morning he had his horse brought in, told his servants to join him, and asked some of his neighbours to come along too. Off they went to Bægisfotshofdi, where Thorolf was buried, broke the grave open, and saw Thorolf still lying there, uncorrupted and with an ugly look about him. He was as black as death and swollen to the size of an ox. They tried to move the dead man, but couldn't shift him an inch. Then Thorodd put a lever under him, and that's how they managed to lift him out of the grave. After that they rolled him down to the foreshore, built a great pyre there, set fire to it, pushed Thorolf into it, and burnt him to ashes. All the same it took the fire a long time to finish Thorolf off. A fierce gale had blown up, so as soon as the corpse began burning, the ashes were scattered everywhere, but all that they could get hold of they threw into the sea.

After that they went home, and by the time Thorodd came back to Karsstad it was getting dark. The servants were milking, and as Thorodd rode past the milking pen, one of the cows shied away from him and stumbled, breaking her leg. They took a look at the cow and saw she was too lean for slaughtering, so Thorodd had the leg bandaged. The cow stopped yielding any milk, and when the leg had set, she was taken out for fattening to Ulfarsfell, where the pastures are as good as the best. The cow kept haunting the foreshore where they'd built the funeral pyre, and she used to lick the stones where the ashes had blown about. There are people who'll tell you that when the islanders came sailing up the bay with cargoes of dried fish, they used to see the cow with a dapple-grey bull up on the mountain side, but no-one knew of any such bull there. Thorodd meant to put the cow down in the autumn, but when they set out to look for her, she couldn't be found. Thorodd had a search made several times in the autumn, but there was no sign of her, so they all thought she must be dead or stolen.

Early one morning just before Christmas the cowherd at Karsstad went to the byre as usual. He saw a cow standing outside the door and realised it was the missing one with the broken leg. After he'd led her into the byre and tied her up, he went back inside to tell Thorodd, who came to have a look at her. They saw she was with calf, so she couldn't be put down, and Thorodd had already slaughtered enough to keep the household in meat.

Early in spring the cow bore a calf, a heifer it was. Then a little later she bore another, this time a bull. The second delivery gave her a lot of trouble as the calf was so big, and shortly afterwards the cow died. They took the big calf into the living-room. It was dapple-grey and looked a really fine beast. Both calves were kept there in the room, the first-born one as well.

There was an old woman at Karsstad, Thorodd's foster-mother, and she'd gone blind. In her younger days people used to say she had second sight, but now that she was getting on, anything she said was just taken as a dotty old woman's meaningless jabbering, though many of her prophecies came true. After the big calf had been tethered to the floor, it gave a loud bellow. The old woman was horrified when she heard it, and said, 'That isn't a natural creature's voice, it's a monster's. You ought to kill the ill-omened beast!'

Thorodd said it wouldn't make sense to slaughter such a promising calf, bound to grow into a splendid bull if reared. Then the calf bellowed a second time. The old woman started shaking and shivering. 'Do it for me, foster-son,' she said, 'kill this calf, we'll all suffer horribly if you let it live.'

'Since you want it so badly, foster-mother,' said Thorodd, 'we'll put the calf down.'

Both calves were then taken out. Thorodd had the heifer slaughtered and the bull-calf taken into the barn, but he gave strict instructions that no-one must tell the old woman the big calf was still alive. Every day the calf grew bigger and bigger, so that in the spring, when the calves were put out to graze, it was already as big as those born at the beginning of winter. The moment it was freed the calf started racing all over the home meadow bellowing as loudly as an old bull, and the people inside heard it clearly. 'So the monster calf hasn't been destroyed yet,' said the old woman. 'We'll suffer a worse calamity because of him than any of you can imagine.'

The calf went on growing, and grazed in the home meadow all summer. By autumn it had grown bigger than any yearling bull, and was a fine-looking beast with magnificent horns. They called it Glæsir. In two years it had grown to the size of a five-year-old ox. It was always kept near the farm with the milch-cows, and every time it bellowed it sounded terrifying. The old woman was scared out of her wits whenever she heard it.

When Glæsir was four years old, he wouldn't let himself be driven by women or children or youngsters, and even when grown men came near, he used to raise his head and seemed ready to set on them. But whenever they persisted, he would just give in and walk away.

One day Glæsir came to the milking-pen and bellowed so loud, people in the house thought it was standing close by them.

Thorodd and the old woman were in the living-room and she gave a heavy sigh. 'You didn't take any notice of my warning to have the bull destroyed, foster-son,' she said.

'Cheer up, foster-mother,' said Thorodd. 'Glæsir's only to live till autumn. Once he's been fattened over summer we'll kill him.'

'That will be too late,' she said.

'I don't see what you mean,' said Thorodd.

While they were arguing about it, the bull let out an even more fearsome bellow than usual, and the old woman made this verse:

> *'The bull's head lashes out,*
> *bellows an omen;*
> *he'll steal a human life,*
> *says my old white head.*
> *The ox will soon guide you*
> *to the grave-scarred earth.*
> *I see him binding you*
> *in bonds of death.'*

'You're a daft old woman,' said Thorodd, 'you can't see anything of the sort.'

She said:

> *'Whatever I mention,*
> *you say I'm daft,*
> *but I see the gaping wound,*
> *gore-drenched the body.*
> *The bull will end your life,*
> *bellowing in anger;*
> *that's what the keen old crone*
> *can see all too clearly.'*

'Foster-mother,' he said, 'it will never happen.'

'Unhappily it will,' she answered.

In the summer, after Thorodd's hay from the home meadow had all been gathered into large stacks, heavy rain began to fall. When the people came out next morning they saw that Glæsir was back in the meadow, and that he had thrown off the wooden block they'd fastened to his horns when he got too vicious. The bull was quite unlike his normal self. He had never interfered with the hay before when he was grazing in the meadow, but now he kept going for the stacks, driving his horns under them, tossing them into the air, and scattering the hay all over the field. As soon as he had destroyed one, he set on the next, raging and bellowing all over the meadow. The men were so scared of him that no-one dared go and drive him from the hay. When Thorodd heard what Glæsir was up to, he rushed out of the house and grabbed a great birch log from the pile of fire-wood beside the door. Gripping it by the branches, he threw it over his shoulder and ran down the meadow towards the bull. When the bull saw him coming, it turned round to face him. Thorodd lifted up the log and struck the bull a blow right between the horns so hard that the log broke at the branches. Glæsir got into a fury at this and went for Thorodd, but he gripped the bull by the horns and tried to swing it round. This went on for some time, the bull charging and Thorodd retreating and pushing it to left and right. After a while Thorodd got tired of this, jumped on to the bull's neck and, with his arms clasped round its throat, lay there between its horns hoping to wear it down. But the bull still kept racing to and fro all over the meadow with Thorodd on top.

Thorodd's farmhands watched the struggle and saw how dangerous things were looking, but they didn't feel confident enough to go to his rescue unarmed. So they went inside to get their weapons, then rushed out again with spears and other things, down to the meadow. When the bull saw them coming it put its head between its legs and with a sharp twist managed to get one horn right under Thorodd. Then it jerked its head so hard that Thorodd was thrown head over heels into the air and landed on the bull's neck. As Thorodd came down, Glæsir gave another jerk of the head and one of its horns caught Thorodd right in the belly and went deep into his stomach, forcing him to let go. Then Glæsir gave a loud and terrible roar and raced off across the meadow down to the river. Thorodd's men ran after the bull and chased it across the Geirvor scree until they came to a quagmire just below the farmstead at Hellur. The bull charged headlong into it and sank down, never to reappear. Nowadays the place is called Glæsiskelda.[1]

When the men came back to the meadow, Thorodd had gone up to the house, and there they found him lying in bed. He was dead. They carried him to church to be buried, and his son Kar took over the farm at Alftafjord. Kar lived there for a long time and the farm at Karsstad takes its name from him.

---

1. Lit. "Glæsir's swamp".

CHAPTER 64

In the New World

THERE WAS A MAN CALLED GUDLEIF, the son of Gudlaug the Wealthy of Straumfjord and brother of Thorfinn from whom the Sturlungs are descended.[1] Gudleif was a great sea-faring trader and owned a big cargo ship. He and another ship-owner, Thorolf Eyra-Loftsson, fought against Earl Sigvaldi's son, Gyrd, who lost an eye in the battle.

Towards the end of St Olaf's reign[2] Gudleif set out west to Dublin on a trading voyage, intending to sail on from there to Iceland, but west of Ireland he ran into easterly and then north-easterly gales, and the ship was driven out to sea first west and then south-west, well out of sight of land. This was late in the summer, and they kept making vows to do all sorts of things if they could get back to land. At last, land came into view. It seemed very large, but they'd no idea what country it could be. Gudleif and his crew decided to put in, not wanting to struggle against the sea any longer. They found a safe harbour, and after a little while some people came down to meet them. They didn't know who the

---

1. The Sturlungs were the 13th-century descendants of STURLA THORDARSON (d. 1183: see also p. 198), particularly his sons SNORRI (1179–1241), author of *The Prose Edda* and *Heimskringla*, SIGHVAT (d. 1238), and THORD (d. 1237), father of STURLA (1214–84), who wrote *King Hakon's Saga*, *King Magnus's Saga*, and the *Saga of Icelanders*. Sturla was also the redactor of the earliest extant version of the *Book of Settlements*. The Sturlungs were one of the most powerful families in Iceland from *c.*1200 to 1262.   2. St Olaf was ruler of Norway 1018–30.

inhabitants were, but they seemed to be talking Irish. Soon a great crowd gathered there, hundreds of them. They attacked the crew, took them all prisoner, shackled them, and marched them some distance inland, where they were taken to a court to be tried and sentenced. Gudleif and his men realised that some of the people wanted to put them to death, but that others proposed to share them out as slaves.

The people were still arguing about it when Gudleif and his men noticed a group of riders coming up with a banner ahead of them. It looked as if one of these men must be a chieftain, and as they came closer, the Icelanders saw that the one behind the banner was an old man with a head of grey hair, but tall and brave-looking. Everyone bowed to him and greeted him as their leader, and the Icelanders saw that every decision was left to him. After a while he sent for Gudleif and his crew, and when they came before him he spoke to them in Icelandic and asked where they came from. They said most of them were from Iceland. When he asked which of them were Icelanders, Gudleif stepped forward and greeted him. The man gave a friendly reply and asked what part of Iceland he belonged to. Gudleif said he came from Borgarfjord, and the man asked which part of the district. Soon he began asking detailed questions about all the important people in Borgarfjord and Breidafjord, then about Snorri the Priest and his sister Thurid of Frodriver. He followed this up by asking about every member of the household at Frodriver, particularly young Kjartan, who was now farming there. But the natives started to shout that something must be done about the crew, so the tall man moved away from the Icelanders and called twelve of his own people to come and talk with him, and they had a long consultation. Eventually they came back to the meeting, and the tall man said to Gudleif, 'I and my fellow-countrymen have taken some time to consider your case, and they have left it to me to decide what should be done with you. I'm giving you leave to go wherever you want, and though you may think it's late in the summer to put out to sea, I strongly advise you to get well away from here. These people are treacherous and hard to deal with, and they think you've broken their laws.'

'What shall we tell people if we get back to our homeland?' asked Gudleif. 'Who shall we say we owe our freedom to?'

'That's one thing I'm not going to tell you,' said the man. 'I'm too fond of my kinsmen and blood-brothers to let them come here and get into the same trouble as you'd have been in if I hadn't been here to help you. I've lived so many years, I expect old age will get the better of me any moment now. And even if I live on a bit longer, there are still people here more powerful than I am, and they'd not show any mercy to strangers. But just now they happen not to be around here.'

The old man had their ship made ready and stayed with them until they got a favourable wind to take them out to sea. Before he and Gudleif parted, he took a gold ring from his finger and gave it to Gudleif along with a magnificent sword. Then he said, 'If you're lucky enough to get back to your homeland, give this sword to Kjartan, the farmer at Frodriver, and the ring to his mother Thurid.'

'What shall I tell them,' asked Gudleif, 'about the man who sent them these gifts?'

'Tell them that he's a better friend of the housewife at Frodriver than of her brother the chieftain at Helgafell. And should someone guess from this message who gave these precious gifts, tell him that I forbid anybody to come and look for me, because no one could make the voyage to this particular spot unless he had your good luck. This is a big country and the harbours are few and far between. Strangers can expect plenty of trouble here, unless they happen to be as lucky as you.'

With that they parted. Gudleif and his crew put out to sea and made Ireland in the autumn. They spent the winter in Dublin and sailed the following summer to Iceland. Gudleif handed over the gifts, and people believe this man must have been Bjorn the Breidavik-Champion, though the only evidence is the story we've just told.

CHAPTER 65

Snorri's descendants

SNORRI THE PRIEST FARMED at Tongue for twenty years and had plenty of trouble on his hands while such powerful men as Thorstein Kuggason, Thorgils Holluson, and other dangerous enemies were still alive. Snorri plays a part in other sagas as well. Many people know about his role in *Laxdæla Saga*, where he was such a great friend of Gudrun, Osvif's Daughter, and her sons. Snorri figures in *Heidarviga Saga* too, for, after Gudmund the Powerful, he was the one who gave greatest help to Bardi. The older Snorri grew, the better people came to like him, not only because his enemies were getting fewer and fewer, but also because he entered into marriage alliances with important people in Borgarfjord and elsewhere, and that increased his popularity.

Snorri married his daughter Sigrid to Brand Vermundsson the Generous, but afterwards she married Kolli, son of Thormod

Thorlaksson of Eyr. Brand and Sigrid lived at Bjorn's Haven. Snorri married his daughter Unn to Killer Bardi, but later she married Sigurd Thorisson of Bjark Isle in Norway, and their daughter was Rannveig, who married Jon, son of Arni, son of Arni Armodsson. The son of Rannveig and Jon was Vidkunn of Bjark Isle, one of the noblest of all the landed men in Norway. Snorri married his daughter Thordis to Bolli Bollason, and the Gilsbakki people are descended from them. Snorri married his daughter Hallbera to Thord, son of Sturla Thjodreksson, and their daughter was Thurid, wife of Haflidi Masson. They had a great many descendants. Snorri married his daughter Thora to Cart-Bersi, son of Halldor Olafsson of Hjardarholt, but later she married Thorgrim the Singed and a great and noble line descends from them. All the remaining daughters of Snorri were married after his death: Thurid the Wise married Gunnlaug, son of Steinthor of Eyr; Gudrun, Snorri's Daughter married Kolfinn of Solheim; Halldora, Snorri's Daughter, married Thorgeir of Asgardshills; and Alof, Snorri's Daughter, married Jorund Thorfinnsson, brother of Gunnlaug of Straumfjord.

Halldor[1] was the greatest of all Snorri's sons. He lived at Hjardarholt in Laxardale, and from him the Sturlungs and the Vatnsfjord people are descended. Thorodd was the second greatest. He lived at Spakonufell in Skaga Strand. Mani Snorrason lived at Saudafell. His son Ljot was nicknamed Mana-Ljot and was considered the greatest of all Snorri's grandsons. Thorstein Snorrason lived at Laugarbrekka, and from him are descended the

---

1. For an interesting story about Halldor, see *Hrafnkel's Saga and Other Icelandic Stories*, tr. H. Pálsson, Penguin Classics, Harmondsworth 1971, pp. 109–20.

Asbirnings in Skagafjord and many other people besides. Thord
Cat Snorrason lived at Dufgusdale; Eyjolf Snorrason lived at
Lambastad in Myrar; Thorleif Snorrason lived in Medalfell
Strand, and from him the Ball River people are descended; and
Snorri Snorrason lived at Sælingsdale Tongue after his father.
Snorri the Priest also had a son called Klepp, but no-one knows
where he lived, and we have no record of his descendants, if indeed
he had any.

Snorri the Priest died at Sælingsdale Tongue a year after the
killing of King Olaf the Saint, and was buried at the church he
himself had built. When the graveyard there was changed, his
bones were removed to the site of the present church. Gudny,
Bodvar's Daughter, was present, the mother of the Sturlusons,
Snorri, Thord, and Sighvat, and she said that Snorri the Priest's
bones were those of a man of average height, not very tall. She
also said that the bones of Snorri's uncle, Bork the Stout, had been
dug up, and that they were exceptionally big. The bones of old
Thordis, Sur's Daughter, were dug up too, and Gudny said they
were those of a small woman, and black as if they had been singed.
All these bones were buried again at the place where the church
now stands.

AND SO WE END THIS STORY ABOUT
THE PEOPLE OF THOR'S NESS,
EYR, AND ALFTAFJORD